2

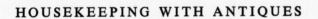

HOUSEKEEPING WITH ANTIQUES

HOUSEKEEPING WITH ANTIQUES

LEE PARR McGRATH

DODD, MEAD & COMPANY

NEW YORK

Second Printing

ISBN: 0-396-06432-9
Library of Congress Catalog Card Number: 70-165673

Printed in the United States of America
by The Cornwall Press, Inc., Cornwall, N. Y.

To my mother,
from whom I learned to love antiques
and
to Aunt Rosa,
whose taste and knowledge inspired us both

INTRODUCTION

This book, a complete guide to the proper care of antiques and other fine furnishings in the home, translates the expertise of specialists into simple instructions anyone can follow. It tells you what to do (and sometimes more important, what not to do) to protect your cherished belongings or to give them first aid in case of accident.

Antiques are always being written about—how to recognize them, refinish them, compare them. This book covers none of these subjects. What it does do is to gather together for the first time advice from the most authoritative sources on the care of a wide range of objects—woods, metals, textiles, glass, ceramics, paintings, prints, and special collectibles such as dolls, firearms, decoys, and scrimshaw. The housekeeping tips here will enhance the beauty and preserve the value of your possessions and will be useful whether you own one antique or a fabulous collection.

Directors, curators, and conservators of major museums and historical restorations in all parts of the country were asked for advice. They replied generously with descriptions of their own procedures in looking after the priceless collections in their care.

Surprisingly, their methods are not at all forbiddingly scientific. More than one curator confided that used diapers make better polishing cloths than any others you can buy. They demolished the old myth of throwing salt on a stained tablecloth (a paper kitchen towel absorbs better and more quickly), and suggested that most housewives wax their furniture too often rather than too seldom. But for all their good-humored acceptance of common-sense housekeeping approaches, there was no compromise in their determination to instruct in the very best methods of preserving period objects.

It is hard to keep from composing a sonnet of praise to these dedicated museum people, who turned out to be the great delight of writing this book. It began as a search for answers to the author's own housekeeping questions, to resolve once and for all the conflicting advice of dealers and self-proclaimed experts. Discovery of the rich trove of knowledge possessed by curators and conservators turned the research into a fascinating quest, and I became convinced that, as in the theater, the most intriguing part of a museum or restoration is behind the scenes.

Finally, I came to share in the feeling of curatorial staff members, perhaps best expressed by John Bivins, Jr., Old Salem's Curator of Crafts, who said: "Collectors must consider themselves conservators no less than museums do, if we are to have any quantity of antiques left in centuries to come. In this light collectors are not simply owners, but responsible people holding antiques in trust for the decorative arts students of the future."

That thought is the reason for this book.

LEE PARR McGRATH

CONTENTS

1. NOTES ON CREATING A HAPPY HOME FOR ANTIQUES   1
2. MAINTAINING THE MELLOW PATINA OF WOOD   13
3. SILVER, BRASS, COPPER, AND OTHER METALS WITH A POLISHED GLOW   35
4. TREATING TEXTILES WITH TENDER LOVING CARE   55
5. LUSTER AND GLEAM FOR GLASS AND CHINA   75
6. PRESERVING PAINTINGS, PRINTS, MIRRORS, AND OTHER WALL HANGINGS   89
7. PERSONAL CARE FOR SPECIAL COLLECTIONS   109
8. HOUSEKEEPING WHEN OUR ANTIQUES WERE YOUNG   125
9. CURATORS' ADDRESS BOOK   137
   (For Repairs, Replacement Parts, and Expert Service)
10. PRODUCTS FOR SAFE POLISHING AND CLEANING   149

Acknowledgments   157
Bibliography   165
Index   167

HOUSEKEEPING WITH ANTIQUES

1 NOTES ON CREATING
A HAPPY HOME
FOR ANTIQUES

Whether your collection consists of Great-Aunt Mary's treasured tea set, a house filled with fine eighteenth-century pieces, or the rocking chair you discovered at your first country auction, ownership is an instant obligation. Antiques are too hard to find (they are the real vanishing American these days) and too costly once found to be treated carelessly.

Even more, the deepest satisfaction shared by collectors is the sense of owning a piece of the past. And no matter how small a portion of history is in your care, there is an automatic dread of damaging it.

Who wants to be the first housekeeper in two hundred years to turn the glowing finish on a Windsor bench into a blotched mess? Or who wants to pay a little too much for a pair of Sheffield candlesticks, only to find at the end of a year that even more of the silver has been washed away from the copper base? "Why didn't someone tell me not to use this polish or that spray?" you may wail, but by then nothing can put back the patina of centuries.

For most of us, improper care of the antiques we are so delighted to find is less lack of will than lack of know-how. But this knowledge does exist. Conservators and curators of such fabulous collections as Winterthur, Williamsburg, and the Karolik Collection of the Museum of Fine Arts in Boston have spent years of study and laboratory research to discover the best possible treatment for the antiques in their custody. And what works for a rare item of museum Sandwich glass will also apply to the more usual daisy-and-button tumbler many more of us can own; a polish that is safe for a Goddard block-front chest certainly won't hurt the charming bargain-priced table discovered in a junk shop.

Why haven't these experts more readily parted with their sound, well-tested advice? Almost to a man (or woman) they note that the care of each antique should be approached as an individual problem—which is hardly a new concept to anyone who has brought up children. "Know your child," the psychologists tell us, but while we recognize that each one is different and common-sense decisions are best, Dr. Spock has long since taught us the value of a guidebook of general rules. So with apologies to that marvelous manual on baby care, let's see if we can outline a similarly simple and practical set of guidelines for coddling our adopted children, the antiques.

How to Know Your Own

It is an excellent idea to find out as much as possible about any antique that you own. If you know whether you are polishing pewter or tin, sterling or plate, obviously you can be guided accordingly. If you know whether a table is cherry or mahogany, maple or pine, and whether it was originally finished with oil, shellac, or varnish, you are ahead of the game in deciding how to care for it today. And you are saved unpleasant surprises if you have been told that a leather-bound book spent the past two hundred years in a clammy Scottish castle; you will then know exactly what to expect if you transfer it to a dry or overheated apartment.

In most cases, of course, it is impossible to trace the life of an antique even when it is a museum piece. The eighteenth-century Philadelphia gentleman who affixed engraved brass plates to his chairs listing the famous who sat on them (presumably shortly after they stood up) was one of the few to attach history permanently to his furniture—and some in our modern age have doubts about his veracity.

What you *can* do, however, is spend a little extra time visiting with a dealer when you've bought something from him. If he thinks you'd like to hear, he'll enjoy telling you all he knows about the piece you've chosen. And it's often surprising how much a dealer can tell you—information he might never have volunteered without your interest.

If you have inherited a family piece, devote an afternoon to visiting with Great-Aunt Nell. She'll adore telling you stories about ordering the chairs for the parlor, or fondly remembering the scent of lemon-oil polish. If she recalls a time when someone decided to lacquer the silver trays, or when (and how) everything in the house was sent out to be refinished, that's just what you want to know, and it's worth listening to several hours of family reminiscences. (Besides, think what fun for her.)

When you draw a complete blank questioning your dealer or your family, don't give up; there are other resources to try. You may be able to take a choice piece to your local museum curator for an expert opinion (inquire about this first, as some museums charge for the service and others don't offer it at all). Sometimes, even though you didn't buy from him, you can query the most prestigious antique dealer in the area; many dealers are interested in antiques whether or not profit is involved for them—that's why they became dealers. Your library probably has style books for various categories of collectibles which will furnish valuable clues to the general customs of the periods when your antiques were made.

And if outside help is totally unavailable, the chapters ahead include instructions for enough do-it-yourself detective work to supply you with most of the information you need to take intelligent care of your antiques. Once you have some idea, however vague, of just what kind of period objects you're looking after, you're ready to go on to the general rules set by museum and restoration specialists.

The Least Effort, the Best Results

The primary and most emphatic injunction of the experts is one that appeals enormously to me—and will to others who share my brand of laissez-faire housekeeping. "Leave it alone!" is the advice of Jonathan Fairbanks, Associate Curator in Charge of Conservation, Winterthur, when asked what he would tell a housewife who has a newly acquired antique. All the authorities seem to agree: "Less attention is usually better than more."

These experts do not, of course, want to encourage owners to neglect their possessions harmfully. What they do want to prevent is our nervous tendency to kill our antiques with kindness. A well-intentioned but inexperienced housewife may do irreparable damage to an old piece in her excess of cleaning zeal. Many of the miracle polishes and potions on the market contain ingredients that will damage period finishes or change their color and general appearance. Every museum authority bemoans having seen some piece of furniture that was "skinned," or silver, brass, and copper that has been stripped and burnished out of any resemblance to the original state.

Even when the cleaning agents in themselves are mild, other pitfalls exist. There is the likelihood of a buildup, particularly in the case of furniture. No matter how carefully you wipe off the excess, a certain amount of wax or oil remains to form a dulling surface film. Heavily engraved and embossed silver is apt to hold polish in crevices. The very act of too vigorous cleaning speeds up the process of wear and removes finite particles of a textile or metal. It is easy to see, therefore, why museums relish the acquisition of a trove of antiques from someone's attic, protected from the elements and sharp changes of temperature, and also protected from the eagle eye and too attentive hand of a super-housekeeper.

However, while caution is in order, there is no reason to discourage the owner who thrills to the process of cleaning and shining her cherished antiques. Advice from museum authorities to "do nothing" is based on the theory that it is safest; when pressed, they will recommend the *right way* to take care of your period pieces, and their suggestions are varied enough to fill happily a compulsive housekeeper's days.

The key point in preserving the appearance, charm, and monetary value of any antique is to protect its patina, which brings us to the important question:

What Is a Patina?

You will hear many knowledgeable people use the word "patina" interchangeably with "original finish," but that is simply careless usage of the English language. Jonathan Fairbanks of Winterthur points out convincingly, "You must realize that the 'original finish' is often gone. What you now have as a rule is the finish that results from centuries of treatment (wear or aged refinishing)." Those centuries of treatment, an almost invisible network of scratches, the resulting translucent glow of color, all make for the indefinable something that brings a responsive glow to the soul of a collector: a patina.

With bronze, the patina may have been induced at the beginning by the original craftsman; it usually manifests itself as green, blue, black, or even red corrosion (depending upon the balance of its elements and the atmospheric conditions it has encountered), and this coloration is greatly prized. Woods, no matter what their finish, take on a rich, warm depth with exposure to air over the years. Old silver acquires a soft luster, unmistakably different from a newly made piece.

Attitude toward the patina is often the dividing line between the amateur and the expert. If an antique has any value at all, a serious collector would rarely have it refinished or replated, no matter how many scars or imperfections mar the surface; he knows that in substituting a modern finish he is throwing away a valuable evidence of age of the piece by removing its patina. This principle applies to almost every category of antique. Overzealous novices may unknowingly harm a period decanter by having the use scratches on its bottom machine-polished into glistening perfection. They may bleach ivory back to its original whiteness, in the process eliminating the soft yellow patina prized by collectors. The cognoscenti feel like crying when some country dealer proudly shows off a cherry table that has been power-sanded and orange-shellacked away from any memory of a patina. A more sophisticated dealer would explain that a chest has been refinished (if it isn't readily apparent) and would therefore lower the price.

Of course there are times—and you must use your own common sense, preferably bolstered with expert advice—when an antique of less than museum value really should be refinished to make its use more pleasant. A Sheffield teapot that is resilvered may be more usable than it was with all its copper showing, and if you acquire a piece of furniture whose appearance is ruined by "alligatoring" or whose surface has been painted or damaged beyond repair, the only sensible solution may be refinishing (with instructions to the refinisher to remove the old finish gently and the old wood not at all).

Oil paintings are the major exception to the rule for guarding antique surfaces. The varnish that is put on a painting is there simply to protect the colors beneath, so when it darkens, as it inevitably does through the years, it is removed without a qualm. The oil paint itself is the surface to be preserved, and masterpieces as well as paintings whose chief value is their age are periodically cleaned and revarnished. This, of course, is work for experts *only*.

As a final note on patina, authorities remind us that there is nothing sacred about centuries-old, disfiguring dirt. In shielding the period surface, it is possible to err on the side of caution, and protect what is no more than a combination of grime, leftover wax or polish, and a general accumulation of soil. Removing this with a careful but thorough cleaning should enhance the patina, not harm it.

How to Prevent Damage Before It Occurs

"A stitch in time" is the best motto you can have when caring for your antiques. Obviously there is no way for a modern repair to equal the quality of age it replaces. Therefore, it is all the more important to avoid problems before they arise.

Don't think, however, that warding off damage is a traumatic affair of constant caution. Living with antiques should be a delight, not a burden. One of the best arguments for collecting them is the knowledge that a dining-room table that has been kicked for centuries won't show much effect from one more generation of children gouging it with their toes. A single scratch will stand out and ruin the pristine surface of a modern coffee table, but it will blend indefinably into the patina of a mellow pine bench. Families who have always owned handsome antiques look on with equanimity when toddlers play hide and seek amid the Chippendale.

However, without allowing concern for your antiques to dominate your life, there are simple rules you can follow to avoid the most common instances of preventable damage. Many of these are second nature to a good housekeeper and obvious even to the rest of us. But according to authorities, their consistent use will go far toward keeping antiques in excellent condition.

1. *Maintain household humidity and temperature at as even a level as possible.*

"About 50 percent relative humidity at 60° to 70° F. is desirable," according to Jonathan Fairbanks of Winterthur. "When the relative humidity goes above 60 percent, you are apt to discover active mold, and below 30 percent relative humidity the spines of books will split." A temperature of 68° F. is often recommended for art objects, but is rather cool for human beings, so a level around 70° F. might be more reasonable. European antiques in particular suffer from the transition to the dried-out environment of the new world, after comfortably damp centuries in the old. A room humidifier is perhaps the best investment you can make to preserve antiques in cold areas where central heating removes all the air moisture; in the muggy South, the same air conditioners used for our own comfort keep collections pleasantly dry. Even a wide-mouthed bowl of fresh flowers kept on a favorite chest will help somewhat to regulate humidity— the water that evaporates into the air is balm to aged wood.

Although humidity level is important no matter what category of antique you own, it affects woods and other organic material in particular, and so will be discussed in greater detail in the chapter on furniture.

2. *Place antiques away from excessive heat or sunlight.*

When you plan your room arrangement, mark heating outlets and unshielded windows as danger spots. A radiator's effect on furniture is devastating: it is both too hot and too dry. Fireplaces have the added hazard of soot, and as antique dealer Sir Humphrey Wakefield of Mallet's of London points out, "You'd be well advised to hang Great-Aunt Agatha's portrait (that you've always disliked) over the mantel, instead of hanging your choice painting there as people too often do." Strong sunlight pouring through an open window will fade mahogany and other dark woods, and the heat of the sun, especially when magnified by window glass, subjects woods to the very extremes of temperature that are most disastrous to it. Antique fabrics fade and their fibers deteriorate in sunlight; for this reason, Colonial Williamsburg tries to keep their more valuable sets of draperies for use in the winter when the sun's rays are weaker.

3. *Think of accident possibilities before they happen.*

"What most people forget is to look at the back of their paintings," the conservator of a major museum reminds us. "They should periodically test the picture cord and screws that hold it. Too many accidents occur when pictures fall off the wall." Preventing this sort of thing will save not only your frames and paintings, but also the prized Lowestoft tureen displayed beneath that might be smashed in the debacle. Antique cups should never be hung by their handles, which are likely to be their weakest point. A fall-front desk should never be opened without first pulling out its supports. Though the hinges will hold alone and unsupported most of the time, if they do give way, the slant top is likely to be left in splinters.

A common mistake among women is to overstuff drawers in highboys, lowboys, or chests. In time, too much weight will break down the drawer runners, which are difficult to repair properly without resorting to screws too heavy for old wood.

4. *Take advantage of all the protection you can get.*

Although a well-waxed table will repel moisture to a certain extent, a wise hostess will keep an ample supply of coasters in evidence. It is far easier to avoid the white circle a drink will leave than to remove it once it's there. For the same reason, plentiful and commodious ash trays scattered through rooms will avoid scars from cigarette burns. Every bowl of flowers should be placed on a trivet—or better still, a tile (a good place to use antique tiles when you don't have enough to frame a fireplace). Somehow it's always the seemingly dry vase that sheds a few droplets of water, and doilies are not enough protection. Heat pads are a must on dining-room tables, and if the finish seems particularly fragile, it's not a bad idea to have a heatproof material under place mats when you are not using a table cloth. Our eighteenth-century ancestors were delighted with the discovery that bobeches (saucers of glass which slip on a candlestick) would protect from the ever-present hazard of dripping candles, and if you have ever struggled to remove beeswax from anything, their use should recommend itself to you, too. A modern idea, but a good one, is to stick felt on the bottom of lamps or display objects that might be scratchy. And of course check vacuum cleaners and electric floor polishers to be sure they have protective bumper guards. Both Colonial Williamsburg and Winterthur ask housekeepers to wear cotton gloves—which protect a wide variety of antiques from finger marks.

To these everyday housekeeping admonitions, curators add some general advice that enters the realm of an overall philosophy for those who collect seriously.

1. *Don't attempt to "glorify" period pieces.*

Dealers will sometimes add a piecrust fluting to a simple tilt-top table in an effort to increase its value, but in the process they actually decrease its worth to knowledgeable shoppers. Although it is tempting to dress up a simple pine chest with elaborate Chippendale brasses, maintaining its original character will better preserve both its charm and its selling price. Never add scrolls, gold leaf, elaborate engraving, and so forth, to any antique not originally so endowed. In other words, don't gild your antique lily.

2. *Don't do anything to an antique that can't easily be undone at a future date.*

This goes back to preservation of the patina, of course, and implies that you will not use polishes, paint, or finishes that cannot be taken off without damaging the surface to which it was applied. You might be in for an unpleasant shock, for instance, if you lacquered a lovely old tray, then later discovered that the solvents necessary to remove the worn lacquer would ruin the underlying patina. From the standpoint of museum personnel, a surface that might be desirably covered for appearance' sake, might need to be stripped at a future date in order to study further its history or composition. And for the rest of us, this rule is a good one simply because anyone can make a mistake—but it won't be tragic if it's a removable one.

3. *Don't let the use of your antique depart too far from the intent of its maker.*

Converting antiques to purposes radically different from their original use strikes most authorities as being barbaric. "A coffee grinder made into a lamp, for instance, isn't a good lamp and certainly isn't a valid antique either," unequivocally states one curator. Turning unexpected objects into planters strikes some people as witty, but makes many others grit their teeth. And nothing further need be said of one lady who reputedly used a china chamber pot as a soup tureen. However, as another curator kindly remarked, "I hesitate to condemn. If someone wants to put the prow of a clipper ship in his living room, complete with running lights—let them. There's enough unhappiness in the world without discouraging someone who enjoys ruining an occasional (and not too valuable) antique."

2
MAINTAINING THE MELLOW PATINA OF WOOD

UNLIKE our contemporary diversity, homes long ago were furnished in almost identical fashion. A man of the Middle Ages or Renaissance could walk into a house with his eyes closed and predict what furniture would be found in the bedroom, great hall, or other chamber—a fact which we can reconstruct today from the fortunate habit our ancestors had of making detailed household inventories and wills.

It should not be thought, however, that rooms were all of one period, which is something to keep in mind when furnishing with antiques. Museum settings, as a rule, are of a single style, historically accurate and planned to best present the characteristics of an era; but they are not necessarily typical of rooms as they were actually used. Only the rich could afford to sweep out and start fresh when new designs came into fashion, and even they must have felt occasional sentiment for a favorite chair or daybed. In the 1500s, for instance, late Gothic pieces must have been used in mellow combination with early Renaissance. Later, American colonists were still listing little "joyned" tables and stools in their wills, although these were certainly considered

13

second best to the newer work of the cabinetmakers. There was often a mixture, too, of so-called "country pieces" and more formal items: a young wife in the early days of this country might set out for the West with a finely carved mahogany highboy from her family securely lashed to the wagon, supplementing it at her destination with simple pine and maple pieces made by her husband or a local craftsman. Although creating a room that looks as if it has grown requires taste and a sure eye, many collectors today prefer such a natural blend of periods, feeling that this makes for a homelike warmth that rigid adherence to a single style cannot help but lack.

This general philosophy does not carry through exactly to an individual antique, though. Gradual additions and changes may add life to a room, but detract from the integrity of a piece of furniture. Curators (and the rest of us) are therefore left with a quandary: what to do about later repairs or restorations, old in themselves but not original, that a piece may have acquired through the years. Furniture brasses, for example, were sometimes broken in use and replaced, or else someone decided to update an old chest with new hardware. A cabinetmaker may have made cavalier additions to a piece of furniture during the years before it was in the ranks of valued antiques. There is no authoritative rule of thumb to cover such situations, so you will have to use your own judgment (augmented with expert advice on furniture of value). An early straight chair later converted into a rocker is often charming and can be left as it is. If a chest has been *recently* refitted with brasses of the wrong period (you can usually tell by marks on the front or inside of drawers), you might replace them, but the original brasses—even if not of the right period—should never be changed. Upholstery on furniture is often a question of taste: an ugly Victorian fabric on a Hepplewhite chair might be exchanged for a reproduction material if necessary, but an upholstery that looks well on a sofa would probably be kept, even if not perfectly appropriate in period.

These and most broad questions concerning the care of furniture can only be given the most general answers by curators and conservators, who emphasize that each antique—furniture in particular—presents its own special problems. "I would never want to suggest treatment for a piece without seeing it," explains Robert Organ, Chief of the Conservation Analytical Laboratory, Smithsonian Institution. With woods, many factors must be considered, among them the kind of wood, the type of finish, and its condition.

What Do You Have?

WOOD The natural colors of wood range widely, and the following descriptions should be thought of as clues, not absolutes. Even more confusing, cabinetmakers were adept at staining one wood to simulate another or just to please current tastes. To make recognition of woods more complicated still, craftsmen were inclined to use them in combination, so experts look for secondary woods in most pieces. (This is among the numerous reasons for considering carefully before refinishing a newly purchased antique; you may very well strip it down to discover that you don't like the appearance of the underlying woods.)

One of the earliest woods used was *oak*—dark, coarsely grained; in Renaissance times it was frequently painted, though today few painted specimens remain. *Walnut*—closely grained and with a natural nutty-brown color—was a great favorite in the Jacobean and Queen Anne periods, and always popular for French country furniture. Burl walnut was especially admired and often used as a veneer. In Elizabethan times *mahogany* was considered a curiosity, but by the late eighteenth century this hard, closely grained wood with the rich reddish-brown color had become virtually the universal choice for fine cabinetwork. In America especially, the two close-grained native woods, honey-colored *maple* and deeper, redder *cherry,* were used for many pieces of sophisticated design as well as for simpler country pieces. *Pine,* usually somewhat lighter than maple and with an open grain, was the frequent selection for informal, utilitarian pieces. *Fruitwoods,* in a range of amber shades, were preferred by the French, especially away from court circles. Dark, rich *rosewood* came into vogue just prior to the Civil War, and many other woods have had their day as favorites.

As important as the wood itself, from a housekeeping standpoint, is the finish. More early furniture was *painted* than most people realize, because so many antique dealers and owners have had an unfortunate propensity for stripping Windsors or other commonly painted pieces to bare wood in the mistaken belief that this would enhance their value. A simple *linseed-oil* finish was sometimes used for country pieces, on anything from fine mahogany to pumpkin pine; it usually has a somewhat softer feel and a trained eye can distinguish it from the harder, sealed finishes like shellac, lacquer, or varnish. Some sort of *shellac* or *lacquer* finish (made from the excretions of the lac insect in India) was more often seen on formal furniture; these finishes sealed the wood and lent themselves to a gleaming polish. An even higher gloss resulted from a *French polish,* which was really a version of a shellac finish. *Varnish* has an undeservedly bad reputation for "checking or alligatoring," probably from nineteenth- or twentieth-century refinishing jobs on earlier pieces that had not been thoroughly cleaned first. Victorian varnishes are often rocklike in their difficulty of removal. Infrequently, you may find *wax* alone used to finish close-grained woods (this was common during the Renaissance, but of course Renaissance furniture itself is not often encountered). *Japanning* (paint, gilding, and sometimes gesso applied to wood) originated, as its name suggests, in the Orient, but soon became widely popular. All of these finishes were subject to myriad variations and "secret formulas."

Aside from finishes, you should be aware of *veneering* (a thin sheet of decorative wood covering another, generally inferior, wood) and *inlay* or *marquetry* (small pieces of wood, mother-of-pearl, or even metal set into wood).

What to Use Once You Know What You Have

Even curators can't be sure every time exactly how a finish was made and applied; experts can be fooled in identifying woods; and only rarely would you know what polishes have been used throughout the lifetime of a piece. So don't be discouraged if the above hints don't help you to identify every piece of furniture. Specialists are right in one sense when they say that you should know all about a piece before attempting to care for it. At the same time, shades of differences required in treatment of different woods and finishes are slight from a layman's standpoint. You will probably be safe if you test everything first in an inconspicuous spot to see if finish or color is disturbed, and if you consult an expert when you have doubts or a piece of unusual value.

In general, curators recommend using a *microcrystalline wax* on most sealed finishes such as shellac, varnish, or lacquer. A caution: wax may soften paint and it should never be mixed with oil, since the two substances can combine into a gummy mess. *Beeswax* and *paraffin* are the most common varieties of microcrystalline waxes. Beeswax is one of the earliest preservatives known, we assume as an indirect result of mankind's perpetual sweet tooth. Honey was used before sugar, and it was soon discovered that the melted comb could preserve many different things. Paraffin is a much less expensive microcrystalline wax that was developed as a petroleum byproduct—a side benefit of the requirements of internal combustion engines.

Though curators refer almost routinely to microcrystalline waxes for woods, because they are both safe and readily removable, in pure form they are quite soft. Most fine cabinetmakers' waxes also contain a portion of *carnauba* wax (a very hard wax that comes from the leaf of a tree grown in an arid part of Brazil —its ability to shield the leaf from extreme heat is an obvious advantage in a furniture wax, as is the hard surface the wax forms on furniture) and *candelilla* (another hard wax, this one derived from grasses grown in the Mexican plains). The addition of these harder waxes is among the well-guarded secrets of makers of fine furniture waxes. In the small proportions generally used, the hard waxes enhance the protection of the pure microcrystalline waxes on furniture subject to household wear and tear.

Nondrying oils are recommended by many curators for use on unsealed or oiled finishes, and sometimes in other special cases. Among the many types of nondrying oils are: *lemon oil, almond oil* (sometimes found in the form of "almond sticks" saturated in the oil), *olive oil, mineral oil, castor oil,* and a great variety of other natural oils. Do NOT use any form of linseed oil when a nondrying oil is suggested.

If an oiled finish is waxed, or a waxed surface oiled, the result may become sticky, and you will have to clean everything off and start over. Turpentine or Stoddard's Solvent (sold more familiarly as household Renuzit) are usually safe for cleaning most finishes, but test first and follow directions on pages 29–30 for cleaning a dirty finish.

General Precautions

WHEN TO REFINISH *Virtually never!* With the unison of a Greek chorus, curators and conservators decry the tendency of amateurs to rush into refinishing. When asked the single most horrifying mistake made by novice collectors, the blunt answer from Theodore Waterbury, Executive Director of the Newport Historical Society, was *"Refinishing antique furniture!"* Vera Craig, Staff Curator of the National Park Service, Department of the Interior, agreed, pointing to "Arbitrary stripping and refinishing and the creation of 'natural finishes'—especially when a piece was originally painted" as typical errors of the nonprofessional.

Serious and unnecessary damage is done to many fine pieces of antique furniture by the owner who is such a perfectionist that he can't tolerate a flawed finish. With the best of intentions, such a collector lowers the value of his possessions through his eagerness to make them perfect. Look carefully at the furniture on display in museums and restorations; you'll see that the marks of wear and age are cherished rather than obliterated with a new surface.

This does not mean, of course, that an antique can never be refinished—only that you should consider stripping as a last resort rather than an automatic first step. As Jonathan Fairbanks of Winterthur asks, "Why scrape down and have a new surface, unless the beauty of the wood is completely disfigured by alligatored varnish? But," he continues, "a surface that destroys the original beauty of the furniture should be removed by a craftsman of recognized competence. Other than as historical evidence, there is nothing sacred about an old layer of dammar or shellac or varnish which is completely disintegrated and is no longer visually pleasing."

If you own an antique and the beauty of its wood is obviously obscured by a finish that cannot be revived, then seek expert advice first, and proceed with refinishing, but don't try to do it yourself unless you are an experienced craftsman.

CONTROL OF RELATIVE HUMIDITY While maintaining an even level of relative humidity is important to the well-being of antiques of every description, it is absolutely crucial when it comes to woods. This was emphasized over and over by conservators. Although metals may thrive at a relative humidity somewhat lower than that required by woods, consider your furniture first, since possible damage to it is so much greater than to metals. An atmosphere of approximately 70° F. and 50 percent relative humidity all year around would be ideal. W. J. Young of the Museum of Fine Arts, Boston, points out that it is stability that counts. "Keep furniture away from fluctuations in temperature and relative humidity," he says. "These raise havoc with works of art. They can stand anything else better than sharp changes."

The most serious problems arise when newly purchased antiques from other nations are brought into American homes. "No other country so overheats its houses," remarks Robert Organ of the Smithsonian. Very similar effects occur if antiques change environments within the country, going from hot regions to cold, humid areas to dry. When winter comes and outside temperatures drop, the inside air is often so overheated and dessicated that furniture literally explodes. Joints open, veneers crack, inlays slip apart, and even solid panels of wood can split. To minimize such devastation, Mr. Organ describes a novel approach: "On arrival, a piece could be put in a sturdy polyethylene bag (like dry-cleaning bags, but thicker) with all openings sealed airtight with Magic Mending Tape—then left there for a year or two. As moisture leaves the wood, it builds up a concentration in the air. Very gradually, moisture escapes through the plastic walls, and the wood can adjust to its new atmosphere slowly enough to avoid great damage." This may seem like a lengthy and unwieldy process to a housewife eager to display a newly acquired treasure, but the extremity of such a solution suggests the severity of the problem.

Concern with relative humidity is by no means limited to newly purchased pieces of furniture. An object may have been in your family for several generations when, during an unusually severe winter, the dry atmosphere causes serious trouble.

Since a controlled level of humidity is so essential to the conservation of all antiques (its importance to categories other than furniture is repeated in every chapter of this book), different means of adjusting moisture in the air should be explored:

1. *Keep a pot of soup on the stove and flowers in each room.* On the simplest level, you can replace a certain amount of lost moisture inside your house with natural evaporation. A vase of flowers is actually just a more attractive version of a pan of water on top of a radiator. Although heated water gets into the air more quickly than cool water does, several wide-mouthed bowls of flowers in a room can add a minimal amount of humidity. Even better is a big pot of soup bubbling on a back burner on a cold day, one of the reasons that housewives a generation ago had less trouble with lack of humidity. According to the Better

Heating and Cooling Council, a large container boiling in the kitchen will add a surprising amount of moisture throughout the entire house.

2. *Lower the temperature of your house or keep one room cool to store your most valuable pieces.* Most people forget the definition of the term "relative humidity." This literally means the amount of water the air can hold at a given temperature. Hot, dry, indoor air will take additional moisture out of wood (air can hold more moisture than the wood can) and the resulting stress to the wood causes extraordinary damage. Trouble arises, particularly in the winter, because as air gets colder, it holds less moisture. When this dry, outdoor air is heated in a house, *relative* humidity plunges (an outdoor temperature of 20° F. and 80 percent relative humidity, for instance, may become an indoor temperature of 75° F. with a 10 percent relative humidity). A cooler temperature, therefore, usually means a higher relative humidity, which is why conservators, like Robert Organ of the Smithsonian, report that furniture often comes to them in better condition when it has been stored in a barn rather than in a house. "We suggest that people put their valuable pieces in places as cold as possible," Mr. Organ advises.

3. *Carefully consider the placement of antique furniture within a room.* The climate of most rooms varies considerably in different areas. Furniture placed near a radiator or hot air duct will suffer more from the effects of both heat and dryness—certainly this is no place for a piece that you cherish. Putting old wood in front of a window through which the sun's rays strike is even worse. Sunlight will noticeably change the color of many woods; mahogany, for instance, bleaches rather quickly. In addition, the sun's heat is trapped in a room by window glass, creating the doubly undesirable effect of a high surface temperature and hot

air around the wood during the day, followed by a contrasting cooler temperature at night.

4. *Invest in a room humidifier or one that attaches to the central heating system.* Other approaches to achieving a balanced environment for your antiques are by nature somewhat makeshift, depending as they do on guesswork results. With a humidifier, however, you can set the humidistat to maintain the desired level, and the machine will go on and off to hold it. If you have extremely valuable antiques, you might also buy a hygrometer with accompanying thermometer, which will give even more precise relative humidity readings. The conservator of a major museum comments, "A room humidifier is invaluable, since wood reacts so tremendously to changes in relative humidity. If a room is kept at a proper level, there should be no necessity for wet sponges in drawers or other home remedies against wood splitting from dryness."

Museums, of course, use large-scale equipment and therefore have little experience with family-sized humidifying equipment. For information on humidifiers that work through home heating systems, write for comparative brochures to the Better Heating and Cooling Council, 35 Rousso Place, Berkeley Heights, N. J. 07922. Consumers Union, an impartial testing service, has surveyed individual room humidifiers and published their findings in *Consumer Reports* (which you can write for to Box 1111, Mount Vernon, N. Y. 10550). Although they have other advantages, most humidifiers that attach to central heating units do not work unless the air-circulating fan is turned on, which usually occurs just to provide heat. Console room humidifiers operate steadily, but vary as to the number of rooms they will adequately service; and table-top humidifiers put out moisture at a much lower rate.

Whatever type of humidifier you buy, you will find that you

have to compromise to some degree between the welfare of your furnishings and that of your house. When outside temperatures become very cold, in most cases you have to lower the output of a humidifier below the level desirable for furniture in order to avoid moisture collecting within the walls of your house and severely damaging them. However, for antiques that are well stabilized, such compromises should cause no major problem.

5. *Air-condition or dehumidify if you live in the humid South.* Too much humidity can in its way be destructive, also. It can cause wood to swell (and drawers to stick), mold to grow, and of course it greatly encourages corrosion. Some equipment conveniently does quadruple duty: heating, cooling, humidifying, and dehumidifying. But there is a feeling among some engineers that such a combination of functions sometimes lowers the efficiency in one or more areas. Individual dehumidifiers and air conditioners do an excellent job of keeping your antiques in cool good order. If you live in a region of great humidity and store small period pieces or textiles in a closet, there are appliances specifically designed to dry out closets. Whatever equipment you have, a hygrometer will tell you the actual condition of your rooms at any given moment.

Special Problems

"BLOOM" Varnished surfaces in particular are subject to "bloom," a whitish haze that often appears because air-polluting substances have collected on the surface. Robert Organ of the Smithsonian suggests trying a gentle rub with a barely damp cloth. It that doesn't work, because the bloom has some other causation, apply a pure, nondrying oil such as lemon oil or olive oil (more on the general subject of oils later). Wipe off *thor-*

oughly or apply a cleaning wax. In the unlikely event that the bloom persists, you will have to take your piece to an expert.

WOOD WORM   These pests are actually the grubs of different wood-boring beetles, and unchecked, they can destroy a piece of furniture. Inspect your furniture for new worm holes from time to time (filling old holes with a wax stick makes this easier) and for traces of powdery sawdust indicating fresh activity, paying special attention to backboards. If you suspect that a piece is infested, take it at once for expert treatment (usually either a fumigation chamber or poisonous insecticide sprays) because wood worm can spread.

Scratches, Wet-Glass Rings, and Other Household Disasters

Prevention is the best approach to all these problems, but since accidents do happen in even the best-regulated households, here are some first-aid suggestions:

SCRATCHES   Minor scratches can usually be blended in with appropriate color, then waxed over to smooth and protect the surface. By far the simplest method is to use a wax stick, a wood-colored crayon carried by most paint stores. (Don't think you can use a shellac stick as easily. Shellac sticks must be melted and applied with expert technique, while a wax stick works like a child's crayon.) The old-fashioned remedy was to rub the scratch with a touch of nondrying oil, in hopes that this would smudge a bit of the finish into it or make the bare wood less noticeable. There is nothing wrong with trying this, if you wipe every last vestige of surface oil away to prevent its causing trouble with wax.

WET-GLASS RINGS   Museums, of course, have little occasion to worry about the effects of wet glasses put down on antique surfaces (though if the current trend to museum parties on the premises continues, they may soon have reason to investigate such hazards). However, curators usually have antiques and accidents in their own homes, where they report some success with the sort of remedies our grandmothers used.

First try rubbing in a little cigar ash, using your fingers, since their warmth and friction help (what to do if neither you nor your husband smokes cigars is just one of life's small problems). The purpose of this is to open the finish to a very slight degree, and consequently it is a technique that should not be used on high gloss shellac or French polish finishes, surfaces readily marred. Next try a sparing application to the affected area of a nondrying oil (such as lemon or almond oil), thoroughly rubbed in and polished perfectly dry. This can be followed with a good paste wax, since a completely dried-off oil on a small spot shouldn't combine with the wax to any noticeable degree. The same general approach is advised for white marks from heat. Deep marks probably won't be helped, nor will black rings, and if you can't remove the marks you should take your piece to a professional, who may find it necessary to refinish the top. There is little point in trying patent preparations, which either contain variations of the above ingredients or some unidentified element with damaging potential.

MINOR REPAIRS   The fact is that there really aren't many minor repairs you can make to antique furniture. Loose chair rungs can sometimes be tightened with a wood-swelling liquid marketed for this purpose, although I must report that I have never had the least bit of luck with it myself. Do not try glue. For one thing, fresh glue won't hold on top of old; for another, to make what seems to be a simple repair of chair spindles usually requires taking apart an entire chair—clearly work for professionals. Besides, expert craftsmen use special glues, which amateurs shouldn't try to work with if they could get them. You should not even try to replace small broken pieces of veneer or inlay. Instead, tape them in place temporarily and locate an experienced cabinetmaker to restore them properly.

The Great "Feeding Your Furniture" Debate

There is no longer any debate at all among experienced conservators about the expression "feeding the finish," although many antique dealers and self-appointed experts still use the term enthusiastically. "Feeding is frankly a stupid word in this connection," says Robert Organ of the Smithsonian. Jonathan Fairbanks of Winterthur agrees. "When people talk about 'feeding a finish,' I wonder what they mean. Everything is dead, so the surface isn't being fed." Per Guldbeck, Conservator of the New York State Historical Association, adds a technical explanation (in case you still cling to the thought of your starving furniture): "The molecules of any 'feeding oil' are too large to penetrate the intracellular spaces."

The concept of "feeding" has been particularly damaging to furniture when it has encouraged the indiscriminate use of linseed oil. It has always been recognized that linseed oil darkens woods. Now it is known that linseed oil "polymerizes" on the surface of furniture, forming a tough, horny coating that cannot be dissolved easily without damage to the wood. One conservator says firmly, "I would never use linseed oil on any piece of furniture under any circumstances. It hardens and turns black." Winterthur, which has perhaps the most magnificent testing laboratories for antiques in the country, has halted the use of linseed oil. "We try to use materials that can be taken off at a future date," Jonathan Fairbanks explains. "Linseed oil forms such a tough surface that solvents to remove it have to be too strong. If you oil a painted or gilded piece of furniture, the paint or gilt has to be taken off in order to take off the oil."

This emphatic trend away from linseed oil will surprise many accepted authorities in the field, since for so many years it was the time-honored substance used on all furniture. And you should be duly warned against the "secret formula finish feeders" so assiduously sold by some antique dealers; one sniff will tell you that they are largely linseed oil.

Putting out of mind any thought of "finish feeding," you may still have questions concerning the use of furniture oils:

1. *What about the famous "museum formula"?* Variations of a formula for furniture polish published long ago by the British Museum (⅓ turpentine, ⅓ linseed oil, ⅓ vinegar, with a small added amount of methylated spirit) have been widely used by museum curators in the past. Success with this mixture depended upon application: ideally, you put on three parts and wiped off six. Today, however, many research-minded conservators have completely stopped using the "museum formula," because they are not pleased with the film that eventually builds up on furniture. (Current museum and restoration thinking on linseed oil has already been discussed.) Although some eminently responsible curators still recommend museum formula, the trend is decidedly away from it, especially for furniture that is to be preserved indefinitely. You would be wise to avoid it for home use, where it is even more likely to build up and cause trouble.

2. *What do you use to polish a piece with a linseed oil finish?* There is some divergence of opinion among curators on this subject. Many state unequivocally that an oiled piece should never be waxed, or some warm morning in June the two substances may combine into a finish of chewing-gum consistency.

(This would seem unlikely unless a piece has recently been refinished.) These conservators suggest a pure nondrying oil (such as a reconstituted lemon oil or olive oil) instead. Again, the secret is to try to wipe off more than you put on. Alternately, an excellent foam-on polish is available commercially for use on oil finishes. The maker believes that this aerosol polish will give a smooth shine on oil-finished wood, where wax my streak.

On the other hand, equally respected authorities take the position that the oil in an antique finish has long since soaked into the wood and hardened. Therefore, they believe it can be waxed if you choose.

If you aren't sure what kind of finish you have on a valued piece, consult an expert. If the alternative treatments for a linseed-oil finish confuse you, my own feeling is that you are on safer ground with the no-wax approach, although wax may work perfectly well. It is always wise to test on an inconspicuous spot. And be sure to use a pure nondrying oil. Many commercial brands have harmful additives.

How to Thoroughly Clean a Dirty Surface

A major cleaning of a piece of furniture is not a task to tackle lightly. As a general rule, dusting and routine polishing keep woods and their finishes in prime condition, and many items in a museum collection (or your own) have been given such excellent care that they will never need a complete cleaning.

There are times, however, when you find lovely old wood obscured with a heavy buildup of wax or a sticky combination of oil and grime. Rather than rush into refinishing (always the *last* alternative that should be considered for wood), first see if a careful cleaning will do the job.

Cleaning wood finishes without removing them is a tricky job and another subject that is still being debated among conservators. Some people use soap and water, but as with linseed oil, most authorities unite against it. "Water is deadly to wood," explains one conservator. "Experts agree that it causes wood to swell. And white marks on furniture are usually the result of water that has penetrated beneath the varnish surface." Although it would seem that a perfectly intact finish should protect the wood beneath, Robert Organ of the Smithsonian explains, "Water gets into the cracks. And it won't dissolve wax anyway."

In general—and this is a technique that must be carefully tested before each individual application—museums use Stoddard's Solvent (the same product as the ordinary household cleaner Renuzit) or turpentine to clean dirty wood. The first step is to try one of these solvents on an inconspicuous spot. IT MAY DISSOLVE THE FINISH. If there is *any* softening or questionable reaction, proceed no further without consulting an expert. If you are absolutely sure that the finish beneath the dirt has in no way been affected (and that the entire piece is covered with the same finish), you can go on and clean it. Museums often work with tiny cotton swabs, but since few homemakers could devote that much time, cotton balls may be used instead. "The important thing is to dip a ball of cotton lightly into the solvent, then *throw it away* as soon as it becomes dark and soiled, replacing it with fresh cotton," advises Robert Organ of the Smithsonian. Work on one small area at a time and watch carefully for the telltale signs of color removal.

Routine Care

"What everyone tends to forget," observed one expert, "is that it is the polishing that counts, more than the polish." You can look at the beautiful, mellow patina of a mahogany stair rail in an old house and see the results of constant rubbing with hands alone. When you wax, apply as thin a coat as possible and buff vigorously with a soft, lint-free cloth. Almost all spray waxes contain silicones, which tend to yellow furniture, so don't use them.

Surprising as it may seem to overly conscientious housekeepers, too much waxing is worse than not enough. A dulling wax buildup is what you must try to avoid. "About twice a year should be often enough for waxing," was the opinion of one curator. "Though, of course, it's an individual choice, and heavily used surfaces (such as a dining-room table top) will probably need more frequent attention." Jonathan Fairbanks of Winterthur agrees. "Wax as seldom as appearance requires," he suggests. "Wax does of course build up, but a certain amount is removed by the solvents in your cloth in the next waxing."

For everyday care, polish your furniture with a clean, soft cloth (the dirt embedded in an infrequently washed dust cloth can actually scratch a glossy surface). As a clue to appropriate types of cloths, you should know that Colonial Williamsburg often buys their supply from diaper services.

One note of warning: when dusting veneered or inlaid pieces, or elaborate French furniture such as that in the Frick Collection, be very careful not to catch a loose bit of wood on a strand from your cloth. Damage is frequently done to delicate marquetry in this way. Edgar Munhall, Curator of the Frick Collection, also advises caution in cleaning gilt bronze mounts.

Many people try to remove and clean them on their own, using too strong a solution and failing to rinse them thoroughly before replacing. It is safer to consult a professional for such cleaning if you have French furniture that is valuable (and certainly most of it is).

Old Spanish furniture is a special case, and if you own any, by all means obtain expert advice on its care. Dr. Carleton I. Calkin, Curator of the Historic St. Augustine Preservation Board, uses hot melted beeswax "to reproduce and continue original finishes on eighteenth-century Spanish walnut furniture." This is something no housewife should attempt without professional guidance, however. If you suspect that you are dealing with such a finish, try an application of a pure paste beeswax, which may not be totally authetic, but will be close.

Marble Tops on Furniture

Marble tops for tables, chests, and other pieces had a great vogue during Victorian times. For this marble, some curators suggest the same thin coat of pure microcrystalline wax that is advised for most of your furniture, although Jonathan Fairbanks reports that marble is not waxed at Winterthur. "I am not really very keen on the business of waxing marble," he explains. "Perhaps it is necessary in the home, but I have not found it so for my own marble-topped coffee table." A major concern is the protection of marble from stains, since it is, like other natural stones, quite absorbent. Oils in particular are destructive; an oily stain will strike into the marble, yellowing it and ruining its appearance. A great deal of damage has been done by people who were oiling the wood of a piece of furniture (which they probably shouldn't have been doing anyway), and either spilled the oil or set the bottle down on a marble top. Any oil accidentally spilled onto marble must be removed immediately, and an absorbent material like plaster of paris or talcum powder liberally applied. Later the plaster or talc can simply be dusted off.

To clean soiled marble tops, try washing with distilled water and either a mild detergent or mild soap. Use a soft brush, rinse *thoroughly* (traces of soap that remain in the marble will yellow), polish dry. There is also a good commercial cleaner (see page 154). It is important to work quickly to avoid letting solutions soak into the marble more than necessary. Washing a marble bust of any kind is more difficult because the marks of dirty water dripping down may be impossible to remove. The best advice is to start at the top, using solution or water sparingly, then mop dry as you go. For routine dusting of marble, use a soft brush or a feather duster. A cloth tends to rub dirt into the stone.

Do's and Don'ts for Wood

DON'T refinish a piece of antique furniture unless you have tried every alternative—and consulted with experts—first.

DO make arrangements to keep all woods in an atmosphere of even temperature and relative humidity (approximately 70° F., 50 percent relative humidity).

DON'T place your favorite pieces too close to heat outlets of any kind; wood will dry out faster there.

DO use only a pure microcrystalline wax, such as beeswax (except on oil finishes) and apply it in the thinnest possible coat, polishing thoroughly.

DON'T use linseed oil in any form on antiques, since the polymerized surface it forms when dry is too tough.

DO use a reconstituted, nondrying oil such as lemon oil or olive oil when necessary, trying to wipe off more than you put on.

DON'T use silicone spray waxes or polishes; they may yellow your furniture.

DO wax as infrequently as you can to avoid wax buildup.

DON'T leave woods where strong sunlight falls throughout the day; sun will noticeably bleach woods and the intensified temperature change is equally damaging.

DO watch for the telltale powdery traces that indicate active wood worms, and if you find them, rush the afflicted piece to an expert for treatment.

DON'T scrub a dirty or sticky finish with soap and water; instead—and cautiously—wipe it clean with turpentine or Stoddard's Solvent (Renuzit).

DO dust often using a clean, soft cloth (being careful not to snag veneers or inlays); for marble furniture tops, use a feather duster or brush to avoid rubbing dirt into the stone.

3 SILVER, BRASS, COPPER, AND OTHER METALS WITH A POLISHED GLOW

METALS, the curators assure us, are the most durable and easily cared for of antiques. And what delightful news that is to the collector. The bright gleam of copper and brass, the fine glow of silver and pewter, add a needed touch of light and warmth to period rooms. They are one of the most versatile groups of antiques, blending into contemporary interiors with a charming ambience.

Our ancestors often turned metal into objects of daily use, which means that they were produced in large enough quantity to put them in the category of the readily collectible antique. And those same serving pieces, fireplace accessories, and candlesticks (whose flattering light can persuade the most modern of women to regret the invention of electricity), are equally useful today.

Fortunately, the care required to keep your metal antiques in peak condition is simple. The routine precautions in this chapter will make it easy to preserve both the beauty and value of your possessions, leaving ample time, if you chose, to indulge in the pleasantly sensuous task of rubbing a beautiful patina to perfection. Though you may have been warned of such obscure ills as tin pest or bronze disease, you'll find that these are far less pervasive complaints than most people imagine.

SILVER

What Kind of Silver Do You Have?

SOLID SILVER   Since silver is a soft metal, it would be impractical to work or to use in its pure form, and some alloy is always necessary to give it strength. In England, standards were set governing the amount of permissible alloy as early as the thirteenth century, though of course existing records date back only to the Great London Fire. Early solid silver was called *plate,* from the Spanish "plata" (not to be confused with later "plated silver," which meant a base metal with a silver overlay). *Coin silver* or *Pure Coin* was stamped on many all-silver pieces to distinguish them from plated silver, once that came into fashion.

The name "coin" derived from a practice of melting down silver coinage to make useful items—a custom with a surprisingly practical origin. In those early days, when surplus coins were acquired, instead of being kept on hand to tempt a thief, they were made into objects (often monogrammed) not so easily disposable. While safeguarding his wealth, an owner could meanwhile dine on it. The actual silver content of coin was about the same as *sterling,* a later term. Technically, sterling is stamped on silver with 925 parts silver to 75 parts alloy. However, coin silver, often found in the form of spoons, seems slightly softer and more easily dented, so it requires an even gentler touch in polishing.

PLATED SILVER   Many collectors prefer the special luster of old *Sheffield Plate* to the brighter shine of solid silver. Sheffield was invented in its day, however, as a cheaper substitute for plate; since it was made of a thin sheet of silver fused to copper, it was sold at about one-third the cost of all silver. Today enthusiasts may pay as much for Georgian Sheffield in good condition as they would for solid silver of the same period. The Sheffield process died out with the invention of electroplating, a less expensive way to deposit silver on a base of copper or white metal.

Plated silver, dating from the 1840s, is collectible, too, though not nearly as desirable as Sheffield. The two can be distinguished most easily by color: electroplated silver is whiter; Sheffield has a warmer look and bluish tinge.

Routine Care for Your Silver

The difficulty that must always be kept in mind with any kind of antique silver is that a certain amount of its surface is removed by repeating cleaning (tests have proven a discernible loss of silver weight over a period of time). This is unfortunate in the case of solid silver, and if you're dealing with plated silver, it is potentially disastrous. Connoisseurs appreciate Sheffield when it is "bleeding"—that is, when some of the copper base shows through. But as more and more of the base is revealed, value lessens, and eventually you're confronted with the difficult question: whether to replate—and lose the patina.

Unfortunately, silver tarnishes readily when it is in contact with the air, forming a thin surface film of silver sulphides. Mustard, egg, certain salad dressings, salt, rubber should all be kept away from prolonged contact with silver. Fresh fruits and flowers, if left too long in silver containers, will release damaging acids.

Other natural enemies of silver are ocean air, vinegar, and all forms of sulphur. Therefore, your best routine care for silver is to *prevent* tarnishing encounters with these substances when possible.

There is no reason not to keep your period silver in use, however, and many collectors enjoy setting a table with antique flatware and serving pieces. Tiny scratches from wear simply blend into the patina, and if you clean and polish properly, little damage will be done.

How to Polish

Some commercial silver polishes currently on the market are far too abrasive for antiques. A conservator at a major museum suggests this simple do-it-yourself test for any polish you're considering: "Rub it between your fingers. If it feels gritty, it is probably too harsh. If you notice any little scratches as a result of a polishing, switch to another brand."

Also to be avoided is the type of silver cleaner that depends on chemical electrolysis. In the hands of museum experts, it may be a safe method, but it takes an experienced conservator to handle it properly. Commercially, such products are often described as "silver dip," and they usually remove the oxidation that highlights any design on the silver. They may save you time, but can ruin your silver in the process.

Don't use detergents on silver. They may stain and discolor it. (This is one of the marks against putting antique flatware in a dishwasher. The action of an automatic dishwasher is also bad, since pieces may jostle together and bend or be deeply scratched. As a final antidishwasher note, silver never comes out of its drip-dry finish as well as it would if polished with a soft cloth.)

To clean silver of grease, wash in hot water with a mild soap before polishing.

Museums are virtually unanimous in favor of the new tarnish-preventive polishes, which slow by several months the normal process of tarnishing in open display. These polishes are not only gentle enough to be harmless in themselves, but they save your silver from more frequent rubbing. (And though museums may not have to consider the point, for a housewife the time and effort rescued from polishing is a worthwhile gain.) From the technical angle, these tarnish-shielding products are also good because the finish they create is easily reversible: you can remove it with ordinary silver polish.

Apply your tarnish-proof polish as directed with sponge or damp cloth; use a soft brush, if necessary, to get polish out of crevices; rinse if manufacturer so instructs, then finish with a dry, dust-free cloth. There are also cloths treated with tarnish preventive to be used for routine dusting; these will refresh the tarnish-shielding finish. Above all, use a gentle touch, being especially cautious about the marks. More eighteenth-century English silver was ruined by overzealous butlers who scrubbed and scraped than by lazy footmen.

Silver on Display: to Lacquer or Not?

Most museums are currently in the process of deciding whether to lacquer some of their silver, and if so, which and how. "We'll all come to it eventually," says a curator from Boston's Museum of Fine Arts, thinking of priceless silver gradually wearing away with repeated polishing. On the other hand, the conservator of another metropolitan museum points out one of the problems: "For American silver with a large smooth surface, it is difficult to cover with any kind of lacquer without ruining the esthetics." Theodore Siegl, conservator of Philadelphia's Museum of Art, compromises, explaining, "I feel that I am unhappy with the different way a light reflects on a lacquered piece. But a chandelier or other silver that won't be closely viewed and is difficult to polish might very well be lacquered." The homemaker has the additional dilemma of locating a commercial establishment that would apply lacquer without first machine-burnishing a piece to a high polish, skinning off the patina. Until a more perfect process of lacquering is developed, and now that tarnish-preventive silver polishes work so well, housewives shouldn't consider this step unless they have old Sheffield or other plate that has already lost all the surface silver it can afford. In these cases, consult an expert and proceed with caution. The safest solution is to prevent tarnish without lacquering.

Closed Display or Storage

Keeping silver away from its atmospheric enemies is the best way to prevent tarnish in the first place, and this is possible to some degree with closed display (in a glass-paned breakfront, for instance) or in wrapped storage. Museums have traditionally put gum camphor in relatively airtight cabinets to retard tarnish. Also good are modern moisture-absorbing crystals. If you are using a painted cabinet, be sure that a latex-, rubber-, or casein-based paint wasn't used. These paints tend to increase tarnish, just as vulcanized rubber floor coverings or flue gases will.

Wrapping your silver in Pacific Cloth is perhaps the safest way of all to keep tarnish at bay. Don't use plastic wrap, as under certain conditions of temperature and humidity, moisture may form. (Just look at the holes they have to put in the bags carrots are sold in.) If you were very unlucky, the thin plastic could become welded to the silver—a big problem to remove without damage to the piece in question. It is possible, however, to wrap cleaned and perfectly dry silver in several layers of tissue paper (avoiding the cheap wood-pulp type with a high percentage of sulphite), finishing with an outer wrap of aluminum foil or plastic. Be sure storage temperature is kept moderate and check occasionally, to be sure that air or moisture isn't reaching the silver.

Special Problems

You may be left in the same quandry as the owner of badly worn Sheffield if repeated polishing over the years has worn your solid silver down to the fire-scale. This *fire-scale,* an oxidized surface appearing permanently tarnished, was produced in the original process of manufacture but never shows unless too many top layers of pure silver have been removed. Experts are currently experimenting with methods of eliminating fire-scale, but at present you must either burnish or replate. Neither is ideal, but machine-buffing is the worst, since it cuts through and removes the entire layer of fire-scale, removing at the same time the depth of color that is the most outstanding feature of antique silver. The resulting white, bland appearance will look very modern, as will replating if it is too thick. If you have a really valuable piece of silver and the fire-scale shows noticeably, consult an expert. Then if the decision is to replate, have it done in the manner most closely approximating the original appearance.

Do's and Don'ts for Your Silver

DO use a tarnish-preventive polish (with a gentle touch) to clean silver in use or on display.

DON'T let your silver come into prolonged contact with mustard, egg, cirtus acids, salad dressings, salt, or rubber.

DO use gum camphor or absorbent crystals to keep the air dry in closed display.

DON'T have your silver machine-buffed under any circumstances; if you are considering replating a badly worn piece, get expert advice.

DO keep silver clean, dry, and carefully wrapped in tarnish-free coverings when it is in storage.

DON'T deface marks or touches that will identify your silver's maker and date.

DO use a glass liner if you're putting flowers in silver, aluminum foil as protection under fresh fruit.

PEWTER, BRITTANIA, AND GERMAN SILVER

Which Do You Have?

Pewter was the poor man's silver, and has been in use for centuries, beginning in Britain with the Roman Occupation. It is made principally of tin, with lead, brass, and antimony added in minor amounts and varying quantities. Its weight and duller shine distinguish it unmistakably from silver, and it is an even easier metal to care for. *Brittania* is still pewter, but with a larger content of tin, which makes it harder, thinner, and lighter in weight. Brittania was spun rather than cast, and became very popular by the mid nineteenth century. Later it was used as a base for electroplated silverware. *German silver* was an alloy of copper, zinc, and nickel, which came out silvery white. Pewter melts easily with direct heat; consequently much early pewter, especially American, was melted down for bullets or to keep pace with changing fashion. The early pewter that remains is therefore all the more valuable and deserving of good care.

How to Polish

Avoid overcleaning your pewter; the object isn't to make it pass for silver. A mild abrasive such as rottenstone on an oily rag will do the job, as will one of the commercial silver, brass, pewter polishes. Some museums wash pewter with soap before polishing, though this is a matter of individual taste. The routine is to rub well with polish, rinse thoroughly, then buff very dry. The main caution to keep in mind is that pewter is a soft metal, readily bent, and the marks and touches are easily defaced. Look for makers' and owners' marks under the base; tankards and flagons are often marked beneath the lip. Be careful, too, of the capacity marks on sides of vessels. If a mark is faint, it may be brought out by rubbing with a nonabrasive eraser. Once in good condition, pewter requires very little further maintenance. You will be wise, however, not to leave fresh fruit or flowers to decay in pewter containers, as the acid released can mark pewter deeply.

Special Problems

Collectors talk in hushed tones of "sick pewter" and it is true that a disease called "tin pest" can attack pewter with virtually fatal results. However, according to Dr. H. Plenderleith, world authority in museum conservation, "Tin pest is exceedingly rare. What's called pest is usually just corrosion." Tin pest involves an improper alloy combined with the action of chlorides, and it is something that most of us can forget about.

What the average collector is far more likely to encounter is badly corroded pewter, and in most instances this, too, is an irreversible process. Because pewter pits readily, even when a heavy layer of corrosion can be cleaned off, the underlying surface will be unattractively scarred. So beware of the dealer who promises that pewter in obviously bad shape can easily be "polished up"—let him bring it to shining perfection while he still owns it, not after you do.

If you already own pewter that is badly blackened, and you're sure that it isn't a rare piece deserving only museum treatment, there are several do-it-yourself approaches. Keep in mind that museum conservators almost unanimously oppose the use of harsh abrasives, which will scratch pewter to some degree. If you can remove the tarnish more gently, by all means do so. But in the case of stubborn tarnish, try the following steps, working from gentle to stringent:

1. First try your regular pewter polish, using some extra elbow grease or an electric buffer (with a lamb's-wool pad, not a grinding wheel).

2. A cigar ash is suggested as a mild abrasive by Theodore Siegl of the Philadelphia Museum of Art. Mr. Siegl reminds us that traditionally a ground-up, dried weed (called "schachtelhalm" by the Pennsylvania Dutch or sometimes known as "pewterwort") was used as a similarly mild abrasive to give pewter a lovely soft glow.

3. If that doesn't work, try a little kitchen scouring powder

on a rag moistened with kerosene. This will bite more deeply into the pewter.

4. Next use 0000 steel wool, dipping it into kerosene. If you are still not getting the result you want, add your kitchen scouring powder, and rub your hardest. Do this only after much prior effort and expect quite a bit of scratching that must be polished away later.

5. The final extreme for pewter is boiling in a mixture of lye, something I don't recommend at all for home strategy. The pewter may soften and be ruined forever, the lye may burn you or anyone passing through the kitchen (it is definitely not the thing when children are around). My heartfelt advice is to turn to an expert if you have reached this step. I won't even give the necessary recipe.

The conclusion to any of the above stages is to give a final polish with silver or pewter polish, rinsing and drying very thoroughly.

Do's and Don'ts for Your Pewter

DO be careful not to bend soft pewter or accidentally damage its marks or touches. Though not documented as carefully as silver, pewter can often be dated and identified through its marks.

DON'T be tempted to try a lye bath for your pewter. Leave that to the specialists.

DO polish pewter with mild silver, pewter, or brass polish, making sure it is rinsed and dried completely.

DON'T lacquer pewter. It will stay lustrous in use or on display without any applied coating.

DON'T leave fresh fruit or flowers in a pewter container for any length of time. Use a glass liner for flowers and put aluminum foil under fruits.

DO keep pewter away from high heat, whether fireplace or stove, as it can soften or melt.

DON'T leave pewter or tin in extreme cold as it may encourage any inherent tendency to tin pest.

DO avoid using steel wool (even fine grade) or scouring powder on your pewter if possible.

COPPER, BRASS, AND BRONZE

Which Do You Have?

Copper and its alloys, brass and bronze, have a long history of usefulness to mankind. *Bronze* (copper and tin) was probably the earliest of all metals in common use, lending its name to the period immediately following the Stone Age and preceding the Age of Iron. *Copper* (the basic element) was a principal commodity in the early Cyprus trade, and the Romans frequently minted coins from *brass* (copper and zinc). What most collectors will be concerned with is the brass, copper, and bronze used from the seventeenth and eighteenth centuries on to make candlesticks, bed warmers, and all sorts of utilitarian and decorative vessels. The three metals are readily distinguished by color, with copper the richer, pinker orange, brass a lighter gold or yellow, and bronze usually covered with a patina which varies from green to black. For all practical purposes, brass and copper are treated identically; bronze requires a slightly different approach.

How to Polish Brass and Copper

A lightly tarnished piece of brass or copper can easily be cleaned by several mildly abrasive mixtures. Rottenstone and oil or whiting and ammonia compound are effective, but it is simpler to buy them as a commercial polish than to mix them yourself. Vinegar and salt were recommended in the past, but though cheap, they are a poor idea since any vestige of salt left behind will corrode the copper. The general routine for cleaning brass and copper follows this excerpt from Colonial Williamsburg's Housecleaning Manual: "Have piece to be cleaned free of dust and grime. Apply polish with a soft cloth, and without allowing it to dry, polish surface with a clean soft cloth, making certain that no polish is left in seams, cut-outs and designs."

To clean severely tarnished pieces, the best recipe is to add more elbow grease, since steel wool and cutting abrasives should be avoided if at all possible. A buffering wheel is not recommended either, since it is apt to round sharp edges or blur definition. This, of course, applies to exceptionally fine pieces of brass and copper and reflects the great care museums and restorations take to avoid damage even if it is virtually invisible. But since brass and copper were often used for kitchen accessories, and may therefore be blackened from frequent exposure to fire, the average collector may have a piece so heavily tarnished that a lifetime of elbow grease would not bring back the shine. In that case, find an expert who will do a responsible job of buffing for you. The hours of polishing time you'll save are worth the slight loss of authenticity of patina.

Brass and Copper on Display

Brass and copper will tarnish not only from sulphur, as silver does, but also from oxygen, so the chances of their spending much tarnish-free time are dim. Some authorities think both brass and copper really should be lacquered. None of the waxes is entirely satisfactory as protection, and if a thin coat of lacquer is properly applied, change in appearance will be minimal. However, many museums prefer the more authentic unlacquered look and are willing either to polish often or enjoy a less than shiny piece. The choice is yours, though it may be affected by where you live. In very humid or tropical areas, many conservators feel that lacquering is decidedly required.

Only two cautions: (1) don't lacquer brass or copper that may come in close contact with an open fire (andirons or other fireplace equipment, for instance), and (2) be careful not to scratch the coat of lacquer, since tarnish will start the minute an area is exposed to the air, and you will be forced to have the piece stripped.

Furniture Brasses

Even if you are too much a purist to lacquer brass and copper room accessories, do consider a tarnish-free coating for the escutcheons and handles on your furniture. There is no really desirable alternative if you like shiny hardware for furniture. If you remove this hardware before cleaning, as many museums and restorations suggest, there is a chance of breaking a bolt or —if your house is like my mine—a child may pick up an essential piece to use as a fish hook. On the other hand, polishing brasses or boule work (brass inlays in furniture) directly against the piece will do a certain amount of injury to the wood no matter how slowly and cautiously you work. And "slowly" is the operative word; keeping furniture brasses shined will take up a disproportionate amount of your time (although there is now a cloth impregnated with polish—see Chapter 10—that can be used safely on brasses with less chance of harm to the wood).

Not all furniture brasses, of course, need be shined. You can be guided to a degree by their appearance: if they are old and look as if they never were polished, maybe they weren't intended to be. Typical Hepplewhite and Sheraton hardware, for instance, depends for its effect on a dull appearance and never needs shining. Gilt bronze, frequently found on French furniture, is sometimes cleaned but rarely polished. If you are not sure about your own brasses, check with an expert.

Bronze

The beauty of antique bronze depends on its patina, which shouldn't be disturbed. (A friend of mine received as a Christmas gift from her husband a long-admired bronze figure, which he had laboriously scrubbed and stripped of every trace of patination. He still doesn't understand why her eyes tend to fill with tears when she looks at it.)

Since the patina on bronze shouldn't be removed (and if it's uneven, that's regarded as proof of age; an extremely even patina is probably a fake), it requires little in the way of housekeeping. Dust it when needed, naturally, but if you're maintaining an even humidity throughout your house, you should have little else to do with it. However, it is perfectly acceptable to have bronze coated with a clear varnish if you feel it is necessary to prevent further corrosion (work for experts only).

This copper alloy is susceptible to "Bronze Disease" (looks something like measles, but patches break out in light-green spots), which is caused by chlorides and encouraged by dampness. In most cases it should be treated by an expert who will probably immerse the object over a long period in distilled water to remove the chlorides. Like the Bubonic Plague, bronze disease is one of those ailments that are interesting to read about, but rarely encountered. Few American or English collectors are likely to be bothered with bronze disease; it is much more apt to attack the long-buried treasures a museum might display.

Do's and Don'ts for Copper, Brass, and Bronze

DO lacquer your copper, brass, and bronze for protection, if possible.

DON'T let these metals come in prolonged contact with salts, mustard, rubber, or other tarnish-encouraging substances.

DO put an underlay of aluminum foil beneath fresh fruits if you're leaving them for a period of time in a container of one of these metals.

DON'T lacquer fireplace equipment or anything likely to come in direct contact with fire.

DO change the water daily if you have flowers in a copper, brass, or bronze container. Best is to put a smaller glass container inside first.

DON'T worry about bronze disease. You would probably have to visit a museum to see it (and there it would be buried in the treatment rooms).

DO remember that since ammonia is used to etch bronze, it is an unwise cleaning agent for it.

IRON, STEEL, AND TIN

Which Do You Have?

Iron is one of the "base metals," which seems a rather demeaning reference to a category that was life or death to early civilizations (how would you like to oppose iron weapons with stone?) and which in later centuries was engraved as carefully as jewelry. *Steel,* that stronger, harder, shinier version of iron, was made into elaborately decorated snuffboxes, jewelry caskets, scissors, thimbles, and other ornamental forms as well as the more expected useful objects. *Wrought iron* (grainier than the later cast iron and usually marked by the forge) was turned into weathervanes, fireplace accessories, trivets, and keys (which a collector might find dating as early as Roman times, and in considerable numbers, indicating man's eternal distrust of his neighbor). *Cast iron* (hard and brittle with a smoother surface) was made in Europe as early as the 1300s, but it wasn't until the middle of the nineteenth century that it became the virtually universal replacement for wrought iron. Cast iron, too, was made into the full gamut of objects from furniture to toothpick holders. *Tin,* although an entirely separate element, is often thought of along with iron because early "tinware" was frequently made from thin sheets of tin-plated iron. In general, all these metals are treated similarly, so individual identification isn't vital.

How to Clean

Rust is the major enemy of iron, steel, and tin, and though slow, it is extremely sure. Unchecked, rust will eat away until the entire object disintegrates. Paradoxically, if you maintain a low relative humidity, you can usually stabilize the rust so that corrosion isn't active and no further destruction takes place. This leaves you a choice: if you think polishing will only emphasize an eroded surface, you can leave the rust and treat the object to prevent further damage; or you can clean it back to a proximity of its original state. The authorities take no position on this, so it is up to you.

Here are the usual steps to clean iron or steel:

1. Wash with warm water and a little mild detergent.

2. Scrub with kerosene or turpentine to remove any oils or grease.

3. Polish with steel wool or aluminum oxide paper (Tri-M-ite), using grits of 600 or 400. If you want to remove rust, you can combine a commercial rust-removing liquid with this step (be sure to wear rubber gloves or your hands will be a mess).

4. Rinse thoroughly, dry with a cloth, then let sit in your oven at *lowest* heat (not more than 200°) for an hour or so to dry out completely.

How to Store or Maintain

Some museum curators are devoted to a mixture of turpentine and Vaseline (the turpentine is added to cut the Vaseline to workable consistency) to preserve their iron, tin, or steel objects. It is effective in preventing rust, but museums have the staff to wipe off fingerprints every time someone touches a suit of armor, and though few homemakers have armor to worry about, neither do they have the time to run around wiping off marks. The turpentine and Vaseline mixture tends to attract dust as well as fingerprints.

Never use linseed oil on iron or tin, because it polymerizes and forms a hard surface that is virtually impossible to remove. Best protective agent is a good, hard paste wax or shoe polish. Some shoe polishes contain water and tannic acid, so check the label and avoid these. Use a clear shoe polish or a car wax, let dry twenty minutes before polishing, wipe thoroughly, and apply two or three times to build up a good, hard coat. Once this treatment is complete, you will need to do little more than dust. However, as Theodore Siegl of the Philadelphia Museum of Art notes, "This will protect but eventually soften. It's just like a shoe shine —good for a day unless you walk through the water. In summer when there is more humidity, you must expect more corrosion."

For wrought iron, any of the old-fashioned stove polishes (usually black graphite with petroleum oil) will give color and a pleasant sheen. If black shoe polish (or wax) is used, the effect is initally the same, but the surface may soon take on an undesirable look of having been painted.

If you live in a humid climate, an air conditioner or a dehumidifier is a worthwhile investment to help keep these metals from corroding. White cotton gloves (like Colonial Williamsburg issues) will also protect polished iron or steel from moist fingerprints.

Special Problems

"Tin pest," as was explained in connection with pewter, is uncommon, and what most people call tin disease is nothing but corrosion. In the rare case that is true tin pest, the metal becomes powdery and the elements go into an imbalance that is irremedial. But you can forget it, since you are unlikely to run into it.

Another problem that is more prevalent is *active* corrosion (rust keeps reappearing and feels damp, although there is no outside source of moisture). This must be stopped or your piece will be destroyed, and it requires expert help.

Do's and Don'ts for Iron, Steel, and Tin

DON'T use linseed oil as a protective coating for any of these metals.

DO protect with clear car wax or shoe polish.

DON'T have iron, steel, or tin machine-buffed with a wire wheel unless the objects are very crude and hand scouring hasn't worked.

DO invest in an air conditioner or dehumidifier to keep these metals dry in a humid climate.

DON'T handle metals unnecessarily or else wear cotton gloves; fingerprints quickly turn into rust.

DO use old-fashioned stove polish, if you like, for wrought iron (polishing it thoroughly dry).

DON'T use scouring powder on iron, steel, or tin.

4 TREATING TEXTILES WITH TENDER LOVING CARE

FABRICS are among the oldest antiques known, which somehow seems surprising. We picture prehistoric man owning nothing more sophisticated than animal skins, yet linenlike fiber from Europe has been dated back to the Stone Age. There is proof, too, that wool was in use during the Bronze Age, and that the Chinese were making shimmering fabrics from the silk worm's cocoon some five thousand years ago.

Textiles are as diverse as they are ancient, since spinning and weaving were part of the individual housewife's lot until quite recently. Although great cloth manufactures were demonstrating their efficiency by the early Middle Ages, there was still a thriving cottage industry, with all the diversity that implies, until late in the 1800s. Wives of early settlers in America expected as a matter of course to produce clothing for their families and simple fabrics to drape their beds and windows, dying them in rich colors with any available nuts or berries. Later, wearing "homespun" (and complaining that it scratched) was the mark of a patriot who refused dependence on Great Britain in every way.

Home weaving, however, could never eliminate the enthusiastic purchase of manufactured and printed fabrics. The output of the famous factories at Jouy near Versailles (we still call their type of print "toiles de Jouy") was always popular. Both before and after the Revolution, English manufacturers were kept busy with orders. Even that less than perfectly devoted husband, Benjamin Franklin, sent to his ever-patient wife "56 yards of Cotton, printed curiously from Copper Plates, a new Invention . . . and 7 yards Chair Bottoms, printed in the same way." He later worried that he should have bought both in the same color.

If you are fortunate enough to own antique textiles of any sort, no matter how shabby they may be, you should delight in your good luck. Think twice before replacing a lovely old fabric on an upholstered piece, even if it is faded or frayed. The value of furniture covered in the original fabric is always much greater. The same principle applies to window and bed hangings or other period textiles; worn and mended, museums still display them with pride.

Curators become very nervous at the thought of housewives cleaning or handling antique textiles. "Old fabrics should not be touched without the advice of a museum-trained expert," is the typical comment of Christian Rohlfing of the Cooper-Hewitt Museum. "*Never* send them to a commercial cleaner without due caution." Old textiles are among the most perishable of antiques, with fibers ready to disintegrate at the slightest improper approach. Often it may be wiser to save old cloth "as is" rather than risk destroying it by careless cleaning or handling. However, there are times when dirt, dust, or fresh stains left on antique fabrics may lead to potentially destructive problems. In the final analysis, you must use your own common sense.

If you have tapestries, coverlets, embroideries, upholsteries, or other textiles of great value and age, they should be treated by a specialist, who will be better prepared for unexpected reactions. If your old fabrics tend more toward the category of Grandmother's quilt or Great-Aunt Matilda's tablecloth, and their value is exclusively a sentimental one, you might prefer to try some of the cleaning methods in this chapter. Keep in mind that the best technique is no better than your application of it, and that you can very easily ruin something in a careless minute that you've treasured for a lifetime.

What Do You Have?

Before you begin, you should try to identify your textile. Is it animal (wool, silk) or vegetable (cotton, linen)? If you can spare a few loose fibers, burn them in a little dish for a simple test. Animal fibers burn slowly, producing a bead and an odor of burning feathers. Vegetable fibers burn more quickly, producing a soft ash and an odor of burning paper. You need to know these "twenty-questions" answers in order to treat your textiles wisely. Animal fibers shrink and lose luster in hot water or chlorine-type bleach; they are also more sensitive to excess rubbing. Vegetable fibers are sturdier, but if you bleach or treat with acidic acid (lemon juice), the treated area must be quickly washed back to neutral.

Special Problems

INSECTS Keeping moths and silverfish away from antique fabrics is much like the familiar household routine of protecting the family's clothes. Nothing should be put away soiled, since this will encourage insect activity. Museums—just as you and I— use moth crystals (paradichlorobenzene) with stored fabrics, sprinkling them over tissue paper between folds of cloth. The important thing is to check these from time to time; when moth crystals evaporate, protection disappears. Spraying moth preventives directly on old textiles is frowned upon by many curators; if done at all, it should be left to professionals who can mist on a fine spray with proper precautions against adverse reactions. Restorations or museums with large collections of textiles maintain sealed storage rooms and fumigating chambers, both obviously impractical for homes. If you own a particularly old and valuable textile, you might want it stored in a sealed container, but this is not a do-it-yourself technique.

MOLD   Humid climates in particular encourage mold to form on textiles. Check frequently for these destructive white furry patches. They can usually be controlled by brushing with a soft brush and airing. Electric closet dryers are available and are a wise preventive measure if you live in a temperature zone where trouble is likely. If an old fabric accidentally becomes wet, quick drying with a hand-held hair dryer is good first aid against fungus growths.

TEARS OR WORN SPOTS   Whenever you notice a rip or a frayed spot that could become worse, quickly catch it up with a needle and thread, even if you are not experienced in sewing. Fabrics of any value should then be repaired by a specialist. The important thing is not to leave a tear, planning to mend it later; in an old fabric, a small break can soon become a major problem.

STAINS   Spills are perhaps the most common hazard textiles encounter. (Why is it that the gravy always seems to drip on a cherished antique tablecloth instead of the everyday place mats?) If a stain is old, it is usually better not to try to remove it. Long-standing ones often undergo chemical change and can only be taken out with damage to the material. But if *you* have made the stain, it calls for immediate action. In most cases, you can take the spot out yourself; if not, a professional can probably remove it. Colonel James W. Rice, one of the country's outstanding authorities on textile conservation, advises, "Take a fresh stain as quickly as possible to an expert. If you can tell him the history of the stain and identify it, he can usually do something about it." Colonel Rice, Chemical Consultant to the Textile Museum, Washington, D. C., suggests writing to the National Institute of Dry Cleaning, 909 Burlington Avenue, Silver Springs, Maryland, 20950, for names of nearby cleaners with experience in handling old textiles.

Covering a stain with salt—that oft-repeated household tip—has no chemical function; the salt is simply a blotting agent. Kitchen paper towels do the same job, and more efficiently. Once you've blotted as thoroughly as possible, consider the value, condition, age, and type of textile to decide whether to attempt removing the spot yourself. If you decide to proceed, experiment if possible on an inconspicuous place. "This is no job for the inexperienced," cautions Colonel Rice. "Even with as many years experience as I've had, I always like to make a dry run before tackling a job in earnest."

Spot Removing Techniques

There are several basic approaches to taking out stains; choose among them to suit your problem:

ALL-PURPOSE STAIN REMOVAL
1. Identify textile and stain.
2. Choose proper solvent from stain removal chart.
3. *Always* test on an inconspicuous spot where all the colors are present. Don't forget the lining.

4. Avoid using too much solvent. That spreads the stain.

5. Use tiniest amount of cleaner on a cotton Q-Tip, lifting the stain off rather than rubbing it in.

6. Repeat, if necessary. But if a stain is stubborn, it is better to give up than to risk damaging the fabric with too much rubbing.

7. If appropriate, rinse treated area to bring back to normal.

RINGING THE STAIN

1. Follow steps 1 through 4 of all-purpose stain removal above.

2. Stretch fabric, stain down, over white blotter.

3. Drop cleaning solvent in a ring around stain, perhaps using an eye dropper.

4. Result should be that the solvent will bear in on the stain from all sides instead of allowing it to spread out.

5. Neutralize, if necessary.

BLOTTING THE STAIN

(For removing candle grease)

1. Cover *both* sides of stain with clean white blotting paper and place a warm iron on top (set on low).

2. Grease should melt and most will absorb into one or the other blotter.

3. "Ring" stain left behind with cleaning fluid (see above).

4. Neutralize, if necessary.

STAIN AND SOIL REMOVAL CHART*

(Technical terms explained in terms of simple household products immediately following chart.)

These soils and stains:	Will probably be removed by:
Acid dyes	1. Alkaline detergent 2. Alcohol 3. Bleach
Adhesives (modern)	1. Dry cleaning
Albumin (egg white, fish slime, sometimes gravies)	1. Digestor 2. Alkaline detergent
Alkali deposits (powdery white stains)	1. Acid solution 2. Rinse in plain water
Animal glues	1. Digestor 2. Hot alkaline detergent
Basic dyes	1. Acid solution
Berry stains	1. Alkaline detergent 2. Bleach
Blood stains (dried)	1. Digestor 2. Hot alkaline detergent
Brown water stains	1. Neutral detergent 2. Mild bleach
Candle grease	1. Dry cleaning
Carbon (black smudges)	1. Dust cleaning 2. Neutral detergent
Clay	1. Alkaline detergent 2. Soak in neutral detergent
Cooking oils	1. Dry cleaning
Copper	1. Mild acid solution 2. Sequestrant 3. Strong alkaline detergent
Corrosion (general metallic)	1. Mild acid solution 2. Sequestrant
Crayons, wax	1. Dry cleaning 2. Repeat
Curds, soap	1. Sequestrant
Dirt, ground soil	1. Dust cleaning 2. Alkaline detergent

* Adapted from a more detailed chart for professional conservators, by Colonel James W. Rice. Colonel Rice's complete chart first appeared in the *Textile Museum Journal,* and will soon be part of a book, *Principles of Textile Conservation.*

These soils and stains:	*Will probably be removed by:*
Dust	1. Dust cleaning 2. Vacuuming 3. Alkaline detergent
Earthy clay	1. Dust cleaning 2. Vacuuming 3. Alkaline detergent
Egg	1. Digestor 2. Alkaline detergent
Finishing agents, oxidized (spray starches, other fabric finishers)	1. Neutral detergent 2. Mild bleach 3. Acid rinse
Food spots	1. Dry cleaning 2. Alkaline detergent 3. Digestor
Fruit juices	1. Neutral detergent 2. Mild bleach
Glue	1. Digestor 2. Strong alkaline detergent
Graphite (pencil)	1. Vacuuming 2. Alkaline detergent 3. Soap
Grass	1. Neutral detergent 2. Bleach
Graying ("washday gray")	1. Alkaline detergent soaking 2. Repeat
Grease	1. Dry cleaning 2. Strong alkaline detergent
Gutter splash (muddy water, very difficult to remove)	1. Alkaline detergent soaking 2. Repeat
Humus (rotting vegetation, also difficult)	1. Alkaline detergent 2. Bleach
Ink (modern)	1. Alkaline detergent 2. Bleach 3. Alcohol
Medicine	1. Neutral detergent 2. Bleach
Mildew	1. Mild bleach 2. Expose to sunlight
Mucilage	1. Digestor 2. Acid detergent
Mud	1. Dust cleaning 2. Vacuuming 3. Alkaline detergent
Odors	1. Vacuuming
Paints	1. Dry cleaning 2. Neutral detergent

These soils and stains:	*Will probably be removed by:*
Perspiration	1. Dry cleaning 2. Neutral detergent
Plaster	1. Mild acid solution 2. Sequestrant
Redeposition (soil redeposited in the washing process)	1. Alkaline detergent 2. Soaking in water
Rouge	1. Citric acid
Rust	1. Citric acid 2. Sequestrants
Salt	1. Neutral detergent 2. Plain water
Scorch	1. Mild bleach 2. Neutral detergent
Shellac	1. Alcohol
Smoke	1. Dry cleaning 2. Alkaline detergent
Starch, oxidized	1. Mild bleach 2. Neutral detergent
Sugar, oxidized	1. Mild bleach 2. Neutral detergent
Sweet	1. Neutral detergent 2. Plain water rinse 3. Bleach
Tannin (nuts, bark)	1. Neutral detergent 2. Bleach
Tars	1. Dry cleaning 2. Repeat
Tea	1. Neutral detergent 2. Mild bleach
Unknown soils	Test for response to all cleaning agents
Urine	1. Neutral detergent 2. Mild bleach
Water	1. Neutral detergent 2. Bleach
Wax	1. Dry cleaning
Wine	1. Neutral detergent 2. Bleach

To use stain removers from this list, always carefully follow procedures described earlier for taking out spots. Steps for complete washing follow under the heading of *Routine Care* in this chapter. Unless otherwise specified, use tepid water, which is more gentle to old fabrics (although sometimes warmer water will speed soil removal). Testing each time is essential, since reactions will vary even when you have used a cleaning agent before. Extremely dilute solutions are safest for old fabrics, and you can gradually strengthen them if necessary.

TERM DEFINITIONS

Acid solution White vinegar (in the bottle it is about 5 percent acetic acid; to use, dilute to 1 part vinegar in 10 parts water). When a "mild" solution is required, add more water.

Alcohol Can be denatured grain alcohol from a paint store, but vodka will work just as well (and might be handier).

Alkaline detergent Washing soda, borax, or ammonia are the most common examples. (A "strong" alkaline would be ammonia.)

Bleach Ordinary household chlorine bleach. A mild solution is diluted with more water.

Citric Acid That familiar friend, lemon juice. You can also buy pure citric acid from a druggist, which is better since it doesn't have the trace of sugar present in lemons.

Digestor Any enzyme detergent such as Axion.

Dry Cleaning Use your own judgment whether to seek a professional dry cleaner or to use a home cleaning fluid such as Renuzit. Do not try to work with carbon tetrachloride at home.

Dust cleaning, vacuuming are self-explanatory.

Neutral detergent Something similar to Proctor & Gamble's Orvus W. A. Paste (see Chapter 10). Use 10 percent solution for testing, 3 percent for actual washing.

Sequestrant Works through chemical action to sequester (or separate) certain staining substances. Calgon detergent.

Soap Any pure soap such as Ivory.

General Precautions

Fabrics of all kinds are particularly sensitive to light. Sunlight fades dyes, hastens brown aging marks, and actually weakens the fibers. Colonial Williamsburg puts away unusually fragile or valuable window hangings during the summer when light is at its most intense, taking them out again to hang in the weaker winter sun. Be conscious of rays from a window that may fall directly on a tapestry or a chair.

Heat and humidity can also be damaging, so plan to keep antique textiles in rooms with controlled temperature and relative humidity. Also give some thought to location of radiators or fireplaces when you place upholstered furniture or hang tapestries.

An important element in museum preservation of antique textiles is their support when hanging, so they won't warp or tear from their own weight. Many conservators take tapestries or other wall hangings down from time to time, rolling them on a tube to "rest." Others back textiles with support strips, stitched invisibly to the reverse side. "At Winterthur, a Dupont sheer crepeline is used to support delicate draperies or bed hangings," explains Mrs. Margaret Fikioris, of the textile curatorial staff in Wilmington. "Or the backing might sometimes be batiste or a sturdier cotton. The important thing is that it be strong, soft, with an even weave. To attach, be sure fabric is totally smooth on backing—then tack."

To Store

When storing fabrics such as table linens, avoid folding. Instead, hang them over wide supports or hangers. Small pieces might be rolled around a tube. It is never good for any antique cloth to be left in creases, doubling the opportunity for abrasive wear. Large items that must be folded should be taken out occasionally, gently shaken, and refolded in a different way to keep creases from forming. Don't try for airless storage (sealing can only be properly done by a professional and is obviously impractical for anything in use). Instead, a light air circulation is better for fabrics. To help prevent yellowing wrap whites in blue *sulphite-free* tissue paper (available at most cleaners).

Routine Care

Dust can be removed from antique upholstery by vacuuming with the upholstery nozzle of your machine set on low (be sure your upholstery brush is washed frequently; hold it slightly above but not touching the most delicate fabric). A favorite museum trick is to place nylon net across frayed and fragile upholstery before vacuuming. Dust comes up through the holes in the net but the fabric stays intact. You can also gently brush dirt off textiles, using a soft white bristle brush. For extremely frail fabrics, loose dust should be removed by blowing it away (does anyone own a bellows anymore?). Draperies, if they are sturdy enough, can also be cleaned by brushing or hand-vacuuming.

To remove a spot from upholstery or to freshen it in general, put a little nonionic detergent such as Proctor & Gamble's liquid Joy in soft water and swish to a froth. Test on an inconspicuous area first. Then take a soft brush (like a shaving brush) and—using only the tips of the bristles—dip it in the froth and rub gently over upholstery. Keep a soft rag handy to remove excess froth and use clean, absorbent toweling to dry carefully.

If you want to wash an old fabric, think twice and consider

the hazards. Any textile is weaker when wet; something that seems perfectly sound in a dry state may tear from its own weight when soaked. Since even experts sometimes have difficulty determining fiber content, you might wash an old cotton quilt in hot water, only to make the dismaying discovery that it was stuffed with wool batting, which would be matted and ruined. Some fabric constructions react adversely to water—Fugitive dyes and highly colored old prints may run, and special finishes (like chintz) may be lost in washing. However, after considering all these factors, you may still be convinced that your old fabric is in good enough condition and should be washed. If so, here are the steps to follow:

WATER-ONLY WASH

1. Use soft or distilled water. Impurities or minerals from other water may lodge in the fabric.

2. Pretest *each* color to be sure it won't run. Use a tiny spot of water in an inconspicuous place and don't forget to test linings.

3. After satisfying yourself that all colors are fast, fill a large flat tub (porcelain, plastic, or stainless steel) with the soft water to a depth of about three inches. Water should be tepid, not hot.

4. Gently lower the textile into the water, supporting it with nylon net. Keep material flat and well spread out.

5. Allow the textile to remain soaking for as long as necessary (not over an hour), changing water when it shows soil.

6. Gently tap off dirt. Don't rub, as most old fabrics can't take much friction.

7. Carefully lift out the textile, using net as support.

8. Without removing the support, press antique textile gently between absorbent toweling, then transfer textile to dry absorbent material as a base for drying.

9. Smooth carefully as it dries, and if necessary, pin edges into shape using fine brass pins.

This wash in water alone may do a perfectly good job of cleaning; a surprising amount of dirt is removed without any other cleaning agent. If not, you may need to add a very gentle detergent to the water. (Museums as a rule use detergents instead of soap, which leaves a scum.)

DETERGENT WASH

Follow the same steps numbered above, testing each color again for fastness (some which won't run in water alone are affected by detergents). Make an extremely dilute detergent solution (for example, 3 percent Orvus W. A. Paste to remainder water) and stir thoroughly. The strength of the solution should be uniform before the textile goes into it. Always rinse thoroughly in clear water to finish.

Do's and Don'ts for Textiles

DO shield textiles from strong light, which will fade dyes and weaken fibers.

DON'T let fragile fabrics hang unsupported; tack linings to draperies, backing strips to tapestries.

DO vacuum antique upholstery with low suction, holding nylon net over worn or delicate fabrics as protection.

DON'T fold old textiles more than necessary; instead, roll small items around tubes and refold large pieces from time to time to avoid creases.

DO consider cautions before washing, then follow directions closely.

DON'T try to remove old stains of unknown origin, but if *you*

have made the spot, deal with it promptly. Either send it to
an expert or use the stain-removal chart in this chapter.

DO help keep white fabrics from yellowing by wrapping them
in blue, sulphite-free tissue paper.

DON'T put fabrics away dirty; this invites insect attack.

DO sprinkle moth crystals (paradichlorobenzene) between layers of tissue paper in stored fabrics to keep away moths and
silverfish, but leave moth preventive sprays to the professionals.

DON'T leave old textiles in rooms where relative humidity and
temperature fluctuate; guard against mold in humid climates.

FLOOR COVERINGS

Contemporary homes are so thoroughly carpeted that it is difficult to realize how recently floor rugs appeared on the scene
in Western Civilization. In Queen Elizabeth's court, floors were
covered with hay. American colonists used "Turkey carpets,"
when they were lucky enough to own them, to drape tables or
walls. For a long time, a bare floor went unremarked in an
otherwise well-furnished home.

Meanwhile, in one of history's curious dichotomies, carpets
had a long record of use in the East. A small fragment knotted
in the basic Chinese technique has been excavated and dated
approximately fifth century B.C. It is assumed that the first pile rug
was made in imitation of animal pelts to insulate its owner from
the cold, damp ground. In both the Near and Far East, fine
carpets were long produced in sophisticated designs and in large
quantities.

Eventually, of course, the West caught on, but even today
there is an aura to owning a fine *Oriental carpet* (which may

just as well be Persian, Chinese, or Turkish) that speaks of the early Eastern head start. Other rugmaking techniques became popular in the West, and needlepoint rugs such as a French *Aubusson* or *Savonnerie* were considered comparably handsome. In England, some of the most beautiful carpets were designed to mirror exactly the elaborate moldings of Adam ceilings.

Meanwhile, there were more modest homes with floors to cover. Then as now, Orientals, Aubussons, and the like belonged to the rich. When the idea of rugs caught the attention of the average eighteenth-century housewife, she set busily to work making her own. Some homes apparently had painted canvas "floor cloths," but so few have survived that they are likely to be found only in museums. More common, and a delight to contemporary collectors because of their individuality and naïve charm, were *hooked rugs, braided rugs,* and *rag carpets.* All three made thrifty use of worn fabrics (usually wool). Strips were torn and woven on a loom for rag carpets, plaited and stitched together for braided rugs, or hooked through a backing for hooked rugs.

Although it is easy to distinguish the kind of rug you own, it isn't necessary from the standpoint of housekeeping because care is—in the main—the same for all carpets.

Special Problems

TEARS, RIPS, WORN PLACES The stitch-in-time credo of curators applies literally and especially to any type of floor covering. A loop or two may pull loose from a hooked rug, an edge may ravel on an Aubusson, a spot may fray on an Oriental—all minor problems unless left untended. Then someone will catch a heel and suddenly you have to contend with a major tear. Even if you are not a skilled needleworker, take an immediate quick stitch when necessary, then have a professional make expert repairs later. Check your rugs carefully for worn backing, loose cording, small holes, and have all these promptly attended to before they cause further damage.

INSECTS   Rugs in use, with reasonably frequent cleaning and moving, should not give you trouble with moths. However, if you are going to be away for a number of months, don't leave your rugs in place. Instead have them cleaned, then roll them, surrounded by moth crystals, for storage in a cold, dry place. Carpet beetles (small, furry insects about the size of a ladybug) are more difficult to deal with at home than moths or silverfish. They love dirt, dark places, and warmth, so avoidance of these will discourage these pests. If you suspect the presence of carpet beetles, rush your rugs to an expert for treatment.

SPOTS AND SPILLS   Refer back to the first half of this chapter for stain removal. In many instances, particularly when it has a pile, a rug will be more difficult to clean than other textiles and will need professional attention.

General Precautions

If possible, you should change the position of your rugs twice a year to keep traffic from wearing them unevenly. Remember that strong sunlight fades rugs as well as other textiles, so keep windows shaded at the time of day when the sun will strike a prized carpet.

Routine Cleaning

Unless it is in poor condition, any antique rug can and should be vacuumed—*if* you use the right kind of vacuum cleaner and the right technique. Never use a beater-type vacuum or one with revolving brushes (rug loops are apt to become entangled). What you do want is a vacuum cleaner that can be turned to low suction; it is helpful, too, to have a full set of attachments.

Colonel Rice, of the Textile Museum, suggests vacuuming your rugs with a brush attachment (some vacuum manufacturers call this a "wall cleaner"). "Don't press too tightly against the rug," he advises. "Always work gently and carefully in the direction of the pile, not against it." A carpet pile, like cat or dog fur, runs in the direction most easily stroked. If the pile of a carpet is distorted by local cleaning, reflected light will be scattered and the carpet will appear to be stained. For less sturdy rugs, use a soft white bristle brush to sweep dirt toward the vacuum cleaner instead of direct suction.

Colonel Rice is dubious about the amount of soil that can be removed by foam or powdered rug cleaners available to housewives, and instead he recommends professional attention for thorough periodic cleanings. Oriental rugs, as everyone knows, must be washed rather than dry cleaned, but this does not imply a home scrubbing. Even museums hire specialists to clean their carpets, and you should check with your local museum for their names or see the listing in Chapter 9.

Would you like to know the simplest cleaning technique for Oriental rugs reported by museums (as a point of interest—not as a guide to follow)? This method was often used by Scandinavian pioneers in America, and surprisingly, there are still a few curators today who believe old ways are best—and throw choice Orientals upside down in the snow to clean them.

Do's and Don'ts for Floor Coverings

DO shift rugs occasionally so they will wear evenly.

DON'T let strong sunlight hit a carpet; it will soon fade.

DO maintain even, relative humidity and temperature for your antique rugs; in storage, temperatures should be even cooler.

DON'T use vacuums with beaters or revolving brushes and remember to turn suction to low.

DO have carpets cleaned periodically by experts.

DON'T let tiny rips or worn spots become major problems. Catch up small tears yourself promptly and have experts make repairs when necessary.

DO take up rugs and store them properly if you will be out of the house for several months.

5 LUSTER AND GLEAM
FOR GLASS AND CHINA

GLASS

OF ALL categories of antiques, glassware is the most popular. And for a very good reason: it exists in such variety that collections can be formed to suit almost any pocketbook or point of view. Surprisingly, there is still a reasonably bountiful supply of old glass, despite its fragility. This is true because a great deal of glass has been produced over a very long span of years.

Something of the magic in turning dull, commonplace substances—sand and ash—into crystalline beauty has always fascinated mankind. Egyptian tombs as early as 1500 B.C. contained glass vessels, and Roman glass has been found scattered along the paths of Empire. At one period, the Venetians kept an entire colony of glassworkers captive on an island to protect their lucrative monopoly. Upper-class Elizabethans, those conspicuous consumers of all time, turned to expensive and breakable glass goblets as proof of wealth when the middle classes began to buy durable silver or pewter cups. A favorite gesture was to smash the goblets when a toast had been drunk.

Today, collectors are about as likely to fling a valuable wine glass into the fireplace with Tudor abandon as they are to dissolve pearls in wine. Instead, they want to know the best housekeeping techniques to protect their fragile treasures.

When major museums have custodial questions about glass, they often turn to The Corning Museum of Glass. Therefore, although this chapter distills advice from many curators, where there is a difference of opinion, the final word is from Corning.

What Kind of Glass Do You Have?

The condition your glass is in is more relevant to how you will treat it than its type, which is fortunate for the nonspecialist because there is a bewildering array of varieties to identify. It is even difficult to be sure you are buying an authentically old piece. The "ring" that is so convincing to a novice has little to do with either age or value. Experienced collectors learn to judge by appropriate color, elements of design, weight; slight streaks, bubbles or other flaws; use scratches on the bottom; and the "right" look and feel. If you're interested enough, study and shopping will soon equip you to talk knowledgeably about blown, molded, pressed, or cut glass, Waterford, Sandwich, Bohemian, or Bristol, and a host of others.

From the standpoint of housekeeping, all you really need to know about classification is:

1. Do you have *flint (lead) glass?* This is an extremely beautiful and brilliant glass, usually somewhat heavy, that was developed in the seventeenth century by adding oxide of lead to the formula. Dr. Robert Brill, Administrator of Scientific Research at The Corning Museum of Glass, advises extra caution in caring for

this glass; "High lead glasses are softer and more easily scratched."

2. Do you have *iridescent glass?* "There are many varieties of this type of glass, ranging from the pre-Roman and Roman periods to the Art Nouveau period of about 1900. The iridescence upon much Roman, and other ancient, glass is the result of decomposition, usually as a result of the leeching out of alkali in the glass by either acids or alkali in the soil in which much of this glass was buried. *Never* wash *ancient* glass having an iridescent surface, or glass with weathering products on the surface. Iridescent glass of the Art Nouveau and post-Art Nouveau periods should be washed very gently as seldom as possible, and should never be scrubbed with a brush," suggests Kenneth Wilson, Assistant Director and Curator of The Corning Museum.

Special Problems

SICK GLASS   A collector would rather hear that the children have chicken pox (from which they'll undoubtedly recover) than discover "sick glass" amid a collection. There is no cure for sick glass. Mr. Wilson describes it as an "inherent vice caused by imbalance in the original glass formula, which causes it to be affected by moisture and humidity." Carry a good magnifying glass with you when you shop, and at least you can avoid buying glass that already shows signs of being sick. To the unaided eye, sick glass looks cloudy gray or white, somewhat like deposit films on healthy glass. But under magnification, you will see that tiny pits and a network of cracks are causing the trouble, rather than a removable film of deposit.

Some museums treat a piece of sick glass by coating the inside with mineral oil which, by filling in the surface, creates a temporary clarity for display purposes. Dr. Brill's objection to this is twofold: (1) the oil tends to hold dust, becoming gummy; and (2) if you want to restore the original surface, oil may be difficult to dissolve. The best treatment for a piece of valuable "sick glass" is to keep it clean and in an atmosphere of more or less constant temperature and humidity. "As far as is known now, a relative humidity of between 40 percent and 60 percent seems safest, and temperature extremes are harmful," according to Dr. Brill. The sick glass won't improve with this attention, but neither will it get worse.

SEDIMENTARY DEPOSITS   To add to the adventure of buying antique glass, filmy deposits are a problem in themselves. Sometimes they are removable, sometimes not, and it is hard to guess what the end results of your cleaning efforts will be.

A number of remedies are used by different curators to clean a cloudy deposit. Your first step should be a careful examination to be sure there are no breaks or fissures in the surface of the glass (if there are, some of these treatments might be harmful). Then try these methods, one of which may work depending on whether the cloudiness is due to a deposit left from the evaporation of hard water or sediment on one hand, or actual surface decomposition on the other. Deposits can sometimes be removed, but surfaces roughened by chemical decomposition or pitting will remain dull as long as they remain roughened.

1. Soak glass for a few days with ammonia and water.

2. Soak a similar time with vinegar (don't dilute, as it is already diluted to 5 percent acidity when you buy it).

3. If you are working on a bottle that can't easily be scrubbed, swish water around in it after adding lead shot, uncooked rice, or cut-up potatoes to loosen the deposit.

4. Use a test-tube brush to scrub, taking great care not to scratch the glass with the metal end of brush.

(With methods 3 and 4 you must consider the possibility that some of the deposit may be scraped away unevenly, leaving the appearance of the glass worse than before).

5. Mr. Wilson and Dr. Brill of The Corning Museum report the most consistent success in removing limey deposits with a product made especially for that purpose, called Lymoff. But they note that aged deposits in old vessels may resist this reagent. Here are the directions prescribed by the manufacturer:

"Dissolve one teaspoonful of Lymoff in each quart of warm or cold water (never use boiling water) in vessel to be treated. Soak lime-coated articles with Lymoff solution at least four hours or more. Lime will dissolve. Rinse with hot water before using. To hasten removal of thick lime deposits in vessels use a stronger solution, soak four hours or more, then wipe out as much of the softened lime as possible and continue soaking with fresh solution." This substance may, however, affect some metals. In questionable cases it is always advisable to consult the manufacturer of any preparation before using it.

SCRATCHES, NICKS, OR BREAKS Sometimes a slight scratch may be polished away with jeweler's rouge on a chamois. This is a treatment to try with caution, testing an inconspicuous spot first, because you may remove the scratch only to have a more noticeable mark from the rubbing. Repairs on glass of any value should be left to the experts. Usually specialists can remove tiny nicks from a rim by grinding (there is also the possibility, though slight, that in so doing, the glass will shatter). An expert can give your glass a professional polish, if it is badly sratched, and sometimes repair or replace missing parts. If you are sure that your broken piece is of relatively little value, you can mend it yourself with a cement such as Duco, which is easy to work with and—unlike the stronger epoxy glues—removable if necessary.

Mr. Wilson and Dr. Brill emphasize that treatments involving the heating of glass objects should be avoided whenever possible.

General Precautions

Following the curator's golden rule, avoid accidents before they happen. Protective covers are a wise precaution when storing any glass, and especially lead glass; remember that glass will scratch easily and don't crowd it.

Avoid sudden temperature changes for any antique glassware. One woman was carefully carrying some treasured old pieces out of a warm house on a freezing day when, to her horror, they spontaneously shattered from the quick change of temperature. Hot water is never advisable for washing glassware, since it may cause the glass to crack. If you use antique glass containers to serve food or beverages, don't put a hot substance into a cool vessel or vice versa.

Since sedimentary deposits are trouble to remove, it is foolish to cause your own. Wine is one of the worst offenders, so wash the dregs from your decanters frequently. Never leave other beverages or food standing for long periods of time in old glass. Be sure to throw out flowers before the stems decay in a vase and change the water daily. Never let the water evaporate in your vases.

Although it is customary to display glass on shelves in a window, where the light can pour through to bring out glowing hues, you should be aware that long exposures to sunlight can in some cases permanently change the color of your glass. If you are not displeased with the prospect of new shadings (clear glass into amethyst is frequent), fine. But to preserve your glass exactly as it is, you should move it out of the sun.

Routine Care

Any glass with a surface that has deteriorated should be washed as seldom as possible and preferably never. Glass on display ought to be washed only when necessary, but dusted frequently. This is both to maintain a pleasing appearance and because dirt attracts moisture, which can be harmful to glass. Objects are usually dusted three or four times a year at The Corning Museum (remember, theirs is a controlled atmosphere), but they are seldom washed.

For many reasons, you should never use an automatic dishwasher to wash antique glass. Hot water, strong detergents, general tumbling are all damaging. Instead, line a porcelain or metal basin with a dish towel as cushioning or use a plastic dishpan for hand washing of antique glassware. Use tepid water (preferably soft), a good detergent, a careful rinse, and a lint-free cloth for drying. The Corning Museum considers clean but old, used diapers the best possible drying cloths—a fairly startling pronouncement to the average young mother who may have just such a treasure trove already on hand around the house while she's saving to buy some really "good" linen toweling.

Some curators suggest a few drops of ammonia in the rinse water to add sparkle, but apparently the chief value in this is ammonia's grease-cutting power (helpful if your collection is housed in the kitchen, for instance). Never use ammonia if there is surface damage to the glass or if the glass is decorated with metal.

It is important to dry thoroughly, especially for decanters or other closed glass containers. It sometimes helps to upend these on a rubber-coated dish drainer before final drying with cloth or man-sized Kleenex.

Do's and Don'ts for Glass

DO change water in flower vases daily and throw out foliage before it decays.

DON'T display glass in strong sunlight for long periods of time unless you are willing to risk a color change.

DO avoid sudden temperature changes for your glassware.

DON'T worry about "sick glass." It is fairly uncommon and you can probably recognize it with a good magnifying glass before you buy it.

DO use tepid water, gentle detergent, and lint-free cloth to wash your glass.

DON'T use ammonia when glass is decorated with metal or when the surface has deteriorated.

DO rinse out decanters frequently, rather than leaving wine dregs to stain them.

DON'T scrub iridescent glass. Don't wash ancient glass, or any other partially deteriorated glass, at all.

DO be careful not to scratch glass with metal ends of bottle brushes or other cleaning tools.

DON'T try to remove wear scratches, a valuable indication of age, from the bottom of a piece of old glass.

CHINA

This category should be called ceramics, but one country—China—mastered the field at such an early age that its name became our generic term. Whether we are dining on dime-store dishes or Chinese Export porcelain, we call it china.

Some people make a broad division between china and earthenware, but the proper distinction is between porcelain and pottery—which includes both nonporous stoneware and porous earthenware. It is quite simple to tell the difference. Porcelain is usually translucent, and you can hold it up to the light to tell. It is also as a rule thinner, lighter in weight, harder than pottery. It looks more expensive, as indeed it always has been. Pottery, on the other hand, is opaque, often thicker and less finely decorated, and most frequently it is porous until glazed.

Potters must be an inventive lot, because through the ages they have created such myriad variations on what is at root a single theme of baked mud (or clay). *Hard paste porcelain,* the finest of all chinas, was an exclusive Oriental secret until the early 1700s, when Europeans discovered how to mix rare clays (kaolin and others) to produce a porcelain of comparable delicate texture. *Soft paste porcelain* was an ingenious later invention, combining glass or glass ingredients with clay for a less expensive, less translucent procelain requiring a glaze. A creative potter named Spode added the ash of animal bones to his clay mixture around 1790 to produce *bone china,* which combined the best attributes of hard paste and soft paste porcelain. Dozens of different beautiful earthenwares and stonewares poured forth, named sometimes for a town, sometimes for a distinctive decorative feature. Everyone copied the work of everyone else and tried to make improvements. There were nineteenth-century bone china imitations of eighteenth-century soft porcelain objects that had themselves been copied from early hard paste porcelain.

What Do You Have?

Although recognizing the distinctions among Meissen, Sévres, Bow, and Chelsea can be an intriguing delight to collectors, it is not necessary in order to give them proper care. You will, of course, use sensible judgment and be guided by the age, value, and fragility of your china possessions when you decide how to clean them. An approach that would be perfectly appropriate for a set of sturdy ironstone dishes might be absurdly damaging to fine Chinese porcelain. In this, as in all decisions on housekeeping with antiques, start with the mildest treatment, and if that works, go no further. It is always better to err on the side of caution, and imperfect cleaning is far better than outright damage. The following questions may help guide you.

Is your piece of china glazed or unglazed? "If unglazed, it will absorb into its body whatever is in the water," explains Theodore Siegl, Conservator of the Philadelphia Museum of Fine Arts. This calls for extra caution when washing. "I would use *water only* to wash unglazed pieces," he continues, "perhaps adding a very small amount of ammonia, which is a volatile gas and doesn't absorb. I would rather not use soap, which becomes yellow as it ages." Other curators report using a very mild soapsuds and water, washing quickly, and rinsing thoroughly. "Never let unglazed pieces soak," advises Leon Rosenblatt, Conservator of Primitive Art at the Brooklyn Museum. "Water may cause softening and later breakage." Obviously, unglazed china should not be used to hold food, since stains will soak in deeply. For unglazed and *unfired* pieces (such as primitive Mexican sun-dried fertility figures), cleaning carefully with a soft, dry brush is the safest course for any but the experts.

What is the condition of the surface? On old china the surface glaze may be worn away or damaged in spots. In this case, you will need to follow the same careful treatment described above. "Crazing"—a pattern of multiple fine cracks in the glaze—also calls for special caution, since any break in the glaze leaves the bisque underneath open to staining or damage.

Is the decoration an underglaze or overglaze? You can easily tell with a close look whether the decoration was put on before or after glazing. When there is no protective coating over the design or gilding, greater care should be taken both in use and washing. Harsh scrubbing will quickly take off a decoration that is applied over the glaze, and even gentle treatment, if repeated too frequently, can remove it.

Special Problems

CRAZING A network of very fine cracks in the glaze frequently appears on old china despite everyone's best efforts. If unstained, this is not a major difficulty, since its damaging effect on general appearance is slight. However, you should remember that a crazed surface will absorb color far more quickly than will a perfect glaze. If you use antique china for serving and it is crazed, avoid mustard, beets, and other strongly colored foods, including those flavored with vegetable dyes such as saffron or curry spices. Never leave coffee or tea standing in a cup or pot for a long period. These are good precautions with any china of value, since even a well-glazed piece might in time be tinged.

To stop crazing from becoming worse, or to avoid it in the first place, keep china away from extreme heat.

STAINS Many stains, whether covering a large or small area, can be removed with a solution of household bleach and water. A number of museum curators feel that such treatment is perfectly safe for any well-glazed china, and suggest soaking in the bleach solution as long as necessary to lighten or remove the stain. Other conservators hesitate to recommend such strong treatment. Mr. W. J. Young, Head of Research Laboratory at the Museum of Fine Arts in Boston, qualifies his approval, saying, "I suppose a bleach solution would do no harm with suitable precautions. I would never use it on a delicate glaze or a fine Chinese porcleain, however." It is also ill advised for hand-painted china and decorations or gilding not well protected with a glaze. Most curators agree that bleaching should not become a repeated routine. Robert Meader, Director of The Shaker Museum, emphasizes this warning. "Use Chlorox solution infrequently. Chloroxed china tends to grow yellow and get dirty again." If you're unsure of this process, try the bleach solution on a cotton swab, testing first on the underside of your china before touching the surface.

BREAKAGE Accidents shouldn't happen, but of course they do, and repairing valuable china is a matter for experts only. These specialists can put together broken pieces with inconspicuous metal brads, the approach most museums used in the past, since display was their only purpose. Or if you plan to use a piece, experts today can probably mend, reglaze, and refire to return your treasure to an approximation of its original state. These are expensive measures, however, and if you have old earthenware or stoneware not of great value, you might try mending it yourself with Duco cement, which would be removable later if necessary. Never use the epoxy glues which are virtually permanent.

General Precautions

When storing china, always put a protective layer (felt or like material) between plates to prevent scratches. Use dust covers (there are plastic or fabric versions commercially available) when china is neither in frequent use nor on display.

If china is being displayed, make sure that plates are set securely in grooves or plate holders. Curators grow faint at the thought of priceless porcelain leaning insecurely in a cabinet. Never hang cups or pitchers by their handles, which are their weakest points.

Routine Care

China that is not in use should be frequently dusted and periodically washed. Even for antique china in actual use, a dishwasher is inadvisable; the water is too hot, and the action of the detergent will quickly remove any decorations applied over the glaze.

Instead, wash by hand in a mild, water-softening detergent (which leaves no residue) and tepid water. A tablespoon of detergent to a quart of water is the proper strength, and this solution should be well mixed before the china goes into it. A few curators prefer a pure, gentle soap instead of detergent; if thoroughly rinsed, this does no damage, but the detergent seems to me preferable. As with glassware, a plastic dishpan or a cloth in the bottom of a basin is a wise precaution against breakage. Never overcrowd; it is best to wash only one object at a time. If you are washing a china figurine, be sure to allow all the water to drain dry. Sometimes water can collect in hollows and weaken such pieces (besides, it is an unpleasant surprise to put a china statue on a perfectly waxed table and discover water drops).

Do's and Don'ts for China

DO make sure that china on display is securely placed where accidents won't happen.

DON'T leave, in your dishes, foods or drink that can stain, especially if there is any crazing.

DO wash antique porcelain or earthenware by hand in tepid water with a detergent.

DON'T use abrasives (scouring pads or powder) on your china.

DO try a 20 percent solution of household bleach to remove stains—but only with caution and never on delicate glazes or fine Chinese porcelains.

DON'T scrub lusterware, gilding, or overglaze decorations.

DO be particularly cautions in the care of pieces that are "crazed" or have a damaged glaze.

DON'T let antique china come in contact with extreme heat.

DO throw out flowers before they decay in a vase; change water daily.

6

PRESERVING PAINTINGS, PRINTS, MIRRORS, AND OTHER WALL HANGINGS

A HOUSE with nothing hanging on its walls would be like a face without features or expression. The character of your home is most definitely expressed by what you choose to hang in its rooms—and the choice is a wide one.

What Do You Have?

Putting aside such rare bits of luck as inheriting a masterpiece (which most of us are far more likely to admire in a museum without need to worry about its preservation), there is still an enormous range of framed antique treasures. Our forebears had their share of healthy ego and were quite fond of having their portraits painted. Some call these, generically, *ancestors,* though they have often strayed from the family where they belong; others refer to them as *primitives,* in reference to hands or other details that are sometimes out of academic proportion. There is a special naïve charm to primitives, a category that may also include pictures of farms, factories, and even business signs—commissioned, perhaps, by men whose pride was in their fortunes rather than their faces.

A less expensive means of self-commemoration was the *silhouette,* popular in America during the early 1800s and made simply from cut-out paper pasted against a contrasting background. Most recent portraiture of all, and barely within the framework of antiques, is the *daguerreotype,* originally intended for the pocket or table, but now sometimes hung on a wall.

Mirrors might be considered emblems of vanity, too, but they also have their utilitarian aspect, and most of us who hang antique mirrors today do so for their value as decoration, not for self-image. They were the starting point for *reverse paintings,* which in the beginning were made in the Orient by scraping away the silvered lining of a mirror and painting directly on the glass. You can easily recognize reverse paintings, though they might sometimes be confused with *transfer pictures,* made by coating an engraving with varnish, smoothing it face down onto glass, then, when it is thoroughly dry, rubbing away the paper backing. A close inspection makes the difference obvious, and from a housekeeping standpoint their care is similar anyway.

Original folk art covers a broad boundary of hanging objects. In the 1700s, the Pennsylvania Dutch had the delightful custom of welcoming new babies with *fracturs,* birth certificates decorated with watercolor angels, birds, hearts, and so forth. Another product of the eighteenth century that is in great demand for contemporary walls is the *sampler.* Little girls learning to sew tried out their fancy stitches in mottoes and later pictures; regrettably, the practice seemed to disappear by the 1830s. *Theorems* were also proof of a well-bred young lady's accomplishments; they were painted with stencils in either watercolor on paper or oil on velvet, and fruit baskets were a popular subject.

By far the largest category of all antiques that might hang on walls is the *print.* Prints were made in profusion, from fine engravings in expensive folios (the Audubon series, for instance) to political propaganda to the ubiquitous Currier & Ives lithographs, well described by Alice Winchester as the *Life* magazine of their day. A great variety of prints that were pages in old books or magazines (such as *Godey's Lady's Book*) can be framed today to great advantage. With such a wealth of choices, small wonder that antiques lovers often find themselves wishing for a few extra walls.

OIL PAINTINGS

General Precautions

Avoiding damage to a painting is the most essential part of its care. When paint falls away, or a solvent wipes off a portrait's smile, it is an irretrievable loss. Since a little time and advance thought can ward off most minor as well as major misfortunes to your paintings, here is a checklist you should follow to prevent trouble.

1. *"Use no patented preservatives,"* advsies Mrs. Sheldon Keck (who is, with her husband, one of the country's foremost conservators of paintings). "These preparations often have non-drying oils which catch dust and they sink down into the structure of a painting adding to its destruction." There is no necessity to "feed" a canvas, even when it appears dry and cracked. What you apply may darken it and be impossible to remove without damage to the paint beneath.

2. *Maintain an even relative humidity and temperature.* This familiar curatorial refrain can't be stressed enough when it comes to paintings. Ideally they should be kept in rooms at about 63° F.

and relative humidity of 58 percent (if *you* are chilly, you can wear a sweater). However, it is sharp change that does the damage, so if your rooms are more comfortable at a slightly different level, keep temperature and humidity constant and you will probably have no trouble. Use extra caution with a new purchase, especially if it comes from a different climate. Paintings are structured in separate layers, each of which may expand and contract individually with atmospheric changes, destroying the bond and in extreme cases allowing paint to slide off into a heap of multicolored dust. Wood is especially susceptible to these changes, warping strongly enough to crack as it responds to moisture. If you own one of the charming early American paintings on wood panels, it may help somewhat if you coat the unpainted back with silicone (some experts believe sealing the wood on the reverse side equalizes moisture absorption), but humidity will still be a factor. If you want to change a frame or add one to unframed panels, get expert help. A frame that allows no room for expansion will sometimes cause the panels to split.

3. *Attach a heavy cardboard backing to your picture.* This is another of Mrs. Keck's invaluable suggestions. Process board from an art supply store or Form-cor works well (you want something strong enough to ward off damage). Once screwed to the reverse of the wooden stretcher, this panel protects your painting from dirt, bulging cords, or even a glancing blow.

4. *Don't leave excess wire on the back of a picture.* Often extra hanging wire is simply twisted back on itself behind a painting. As time goes by, this tangle may push into the canvas, causing a bulge or worse. A backing on your picture as suggested by Mrs. Keck will of course safeguard against such damage.

5. *Check hanging screws frequently.* Surprising as it may seem, more paintings are damaged by falling from the wall than

in any other way. There is no antique value in old, loose screws, rusty picture hooks, or frayed wire. Replace them whenever necessary, checking at least once a year.

6. *Never try to clean the surface of a painting yourself.* Though this seems such an obvious injunction, considering the difficulties a trained restorer may encounter in cleaning, an amazing number of housewives seem to rush heedlessly ahead on their own—usually with dire results. "Women use cut lemons or potatoes to clean their oil paintings," Henry J. Harlow, Chief Curator, Old Sturbridge Village, reports with open horror. "This and scrubbing pictures with soap and water are among the most serious errors amateurs make in caring for antiques." Leave cleaning to the experts.

7. *Be selective in choosing locations where your pictures will hang.* Over the fireplace, that all-time favorite, is probably the worst possible setting for a painting you value. Heat and fluctuating temperatures speed up the aging process there; dirt will be deposited on your picture from both convection and soot. Of course if your heart is set on the effect of a painting over your mantel, go ahead, but realize the hazards and be prepared to pay for more frequent professional cleaning. Sometimes less apparent heat sources cause trouble. Guard against radiators or hot air vents that may send streams of heat a considerable distance to hit your picture.

8. *Make sure that paintings are protected whenever they are off the walls.* When you take down your pictures—perhaps to move or to repaint a wall—they are at their most vulnerable. We tend to think that turning a painting to its reverse side protects the surface, forgetting it can be as easily damaged through the back of the canvas. First, choose a safe storage spot where children or other intruders won't venture into an accident. Stack

canvases against the wall with sheets of heavy cardboard in between (protecting both front and back of the pictures). To keep paintings from sliding, prop the bottoms on pillows or foam rubber pads.

9. *Leave expert treatment to the experts.* Never under any circumstances decide to remove darkened varnish yourself. (Would anyone be so unwise?) This is a job for a professional restorer, and a carefully chosen one at that. Don't try to repair a tear in a canvas, either, though it's a good idea to hold it together with masking tape on the back—*never the front*—as temporary first aid. In the unlikely event that your painting becomes water soaked, that is real trouble. The canvas will first expand, then contract. Rush it immediately—while still wet—to a restorer.

10. *If you use a light over a picture, be sure that it doesn't heat the surface.* There are cool bulbs available as individual lights for paintings and you should use one. Also check the electric wire to be sure it doesn't push against the back of the canvas.

Routine Care

Unless a picture is in excellent condition, its paint firmly adhering to the surface, it shouldn't be touched at all. If you examine it closely without seeing loose flakes of paint, however, there is nothing wrong with dusting the surface when necessary. Some museums suggest a silk cloth, but according to Mrs. Keck, the best duster is a soft brush, about three or four inches wide, in badger or camel's hair. A rag or feather duster might catch in the paint, pulling off tiny fragments. Gently move your soft brush across the painting in both directions.

If the frame is a perfectly simple one, you might go on to dust it with the same brush. But if it is in any way elaborate, it can be cleaned more effectively with the upholstery brush of a vacuum turned to lowest suction. Remember that the frame of an old picture is also very fragile. Examine it carefully for loose bits that might come off and be irretrievably lost in the vacuum cleaner, and proceed with great caution, keeping the suction well away from the front of your canvas where paint could be removed.

The most painstaking housekeeper is in for a shock if she hasn't looked behind her pictures recently. Dust and dirt accumulate on the backs, as well as odd bits of debris—pine needles from Christmas swags, for instance. None of this does paintings any good, of course, and you might clean the cracks with the upholstery nozzle set on lowest suction. Don't scrub, but hold brush a fraction above canvas, first removing any loose paper labels. Move the brush gently across the back of the canvas, but *only* if the paint is firmly adhered to the front of the picture, if the canvas itself isn't torn, weak, or dessicated, and if the painting isn't loose from its stretcher. If you have the slightest doubts about this, DON'T try it. I'm not courageous enough, myself, but would rather have a painting cleaned professionally and the back covered with protective cardboard to keep out future dirt.

If you plan to put a painting with its face down for this or any other reason, it is imperative that you first prepare a place to receive it. A large table covered with clean newsprint (available in art stores) works well. Add cushions or pads to support the frame without damage. Then, if you remove the canvas from its frame (which is not usually necessary for superficial cleaning), replace the newsprint with clean before putting the picture down again. You don't want it to rest on dislodged dirt.

Whether to Clean and Revarnish Paintings

Most paintings were originally coated with varnish on completion to protect the pigments from grime and aging. Often, though, itinerant American folk artists moved on so quickly that they didn't see their paintings dry—let alone varnished. Therefore your paintings may have (1) no varnish at all, in which case an old picture will probably be dirt encrusted and somewhat hard to clean; (2) the original varnish, which usually darkens and attracts dirt as it ages; or (3) a coat of varnish applied at some intermittent cleaning point in your painting's history. In the last case, it is even possible that the revarnishing may have been done with color added to fake the brownish tone of age. During the nineteenth century the "Old Master Glow" was greatly admired.

The varnished surface of an oil painting is an anomaly in the field of antiques. For once, the concern is not with a patina built up through the ages, but with what is beneath: the painted colors originally intended by the artist. This leaves squarely up to you the choice of whether to have a picture cleaned and revarnished. If you love the soft, mellow look as it is (and the painting is otherwise in good condition), there is no necessity to remove the old varnish. If you would rather save the expense—cleaning and revarnishing are *not* do-it-yourself projects—then put it off to another time. But all things being equal, most experts today would agree with Mrs. Keck, who says, "Personally, I enjoy cleaned paintings more than I do those covered with grime and darkened varnish. To me, they are more aesthetically pleasing; they also happen to be historically more accurate documents."

How to Choose a Professional Restorer

Of all experts you might ever consult about antiques, none should be selected more carefully than a restorer of paintings. You are literally putting the life of your picture into his hands. The curator of a major restoration once told me of dropping in unexpectedly on a new restorer working on a minor picture. As he watched, horrified, the face of the infant in a painting of the Madonna and child disappeared forever into cleaning solvent.

There is no licensing in this field to protect the unwary. One museum conservator remarked, "We pick our painting restorers with the same care we pick a doctor for our children—on the basis of the best advice we can get and an examination of other work they have done." Some museums provide a list of local restorers, without guaranteeing their work. You can rely on the restorers listed by Caroline Keck in her excellent book, *A Handbook on the Care of Paintings*. In any case, you should request a written estimate (it may be on a sliding scale) of what your restorer will do. "On anything important—if you are paying over fifty dollars," Mrs. Keck also suggests, "you should have photographs before treatment and after cleaning or repair but before any in-panting." These are invaluable.

Do's and Don'ts for Oil Paintings

DO check hanging screws and picture hooks at least once a year.
DON'T keep your pictures where relative humidity and temperature will fluctuate.
DO have someone stand by in case of accident when you remove a painting from the wall.
DON'T attempt to treat the surface of a painting in any way

yourself; under no circumstances use patented preservatives, and leave cleaning to the professionals.

DO have the backs of your pictures protected with a shield of heavy cardboard or Form-cor.

DON'T hang a painting where direct heat will strike it.

DO carefully dust the face of your canvas once or twice a year using a soft, wide brush of badger or camel's hair—but *only* if the paint is firmly attached.

DON'T let excess picture wire or electric cords bulge behind your canvases; check overlights to be sure they are not heating the surfaces of your pictures.

DO protect paintings when off the wall with cardboard between both front and back and cushions under frames.

DON'T roll a painting unless absolutely necessary, then do it paint side *out*. (As in any other form of oilcloth this produces cracking, but rolling paint side in encourages contracted ridges of the surface which soon fall away in loss lines.)

DO choose a restorer only after careful consideration of his qualifications.

PRINTS, PASTELS, AND WATERCOLORS

These three different art forms are grouped together because their major housekeeping consideration should be the preservation of the paper on which they are made.

However, there are important distinctions. A *pastel* is unbelievably fragile. Unframed, the powdered chalk of its surface can be wiped away with a careless gesture; even protected by framing, the color may shake loose from its background with a fall or a slamming door. A pastel must be well separated from its glass, to which the colored powders may otherwise adhere. It shouldn't be framed in plexiglas at all; the resulting increased static electricity will intensify this problem. In a humid climate, pastels tend to attract mold, but this usually can be avoided with air conditioning or humidity control. An expert might add a backing treated with a fungicidal preparation, but these are poisonous and definitely not for household handling. The pastel itself can never be cleaned, and no one but a specialist in paper conservation should touch it.

Watercolors are delicate, too, but fortunately not to the same degree as pastels. Light is particularly damaging to a watercolor, which will fade noticeably in a short time if hung where strong sunlight hits it. Artifical light can also be harmful, and general aging will be hastened by heat or moisture. Don't forget that although an old watercolor has been dry for a long time, the colors can still be dissolved if the painting gets wet.

Since as a rule prints are more stable than watercolors and pastels, they are cared for primarily from the viewpoint of preserving the paper on which they are made. In the case of *silhouettes,* the entire art medium is paper, so this approach holds even more true. Some of the suggestions that follow apply specifically to prints, but most are equally applicable to watercolors, pastels, silhouettes, or other art forms on paper backgrounds.

Mrs. Christa Gaehde, nationally known specialist in the conservation of paper, cautions, "Paper should be handled as little as possible. Great damage can easily be done with simple procedures if you don't have experience using them. A print can be ruined forever in just a few minutes."

General Precautions

Light, heat, and humidity are the great aging enemies of paper. Depending on the composition of the paper, they will cause it to turn brown at a slower or faster rate. There is no point in trying to return paper to its original pristine condition; this would spoil it completely. But you should try to avoid further deterioration. Keep rooms where pictures hang at an even level of cool temperature and low humidity. Unless you have air conditioning, it's a wise idea to glue small pieces of cork behind the four corners of frames to allow air to circulate.

Check the backs of your pictures and remove old, stained backing papers (if not attached to print itself—detaching a print requires an expert). At best these attract insects, and at worst their stains will gradually be absorbed into your print. Wood was commonly used behind prints in the past and it should be replaced, too. The resin or acid from the wood can seep through several layers to penetrate to the front. Corrgated cardboard is especially bad. It can eventually cause ridges on the face of your print and this discolored ridging is particularly hard to remove. All this old backing material should be replaced with museum-quality board (100 percent rag fiber), and sealed to keep out dust.

Art on paper should not be rolled for storage, and of course should never be folded or creased. Don't trim or cut margins; this destroys a great deal of the value.

If you are having a picture newly matted and framed, keep in mind these points:

MATTING

1. For new matting, insist on 100 percent rag fiber mat stock. The small difference in price is worthwhile because cheaper mats

may stain the print or encourage bacteria, leading to "foxing" and "mildew."

2. If you are using an old mat because of its decorative values, you should replace the rear board with new museum-quality board. If your print is very valuable, ask an expert if a thin rag board strip should be invisibly inserted between print and the old mat for protection.

3. Mats are available in thicknesses of 1 ply, 2 ply, 4 ply. Although it costs a little more, 4 ply is best. A small print might get by with 2 ply, but 4 ply is essential for large prints requiring strong support. Never use 1 ply.

4. Never dry-mount or paste a print, watercolor, or pastel to any support. Art on paper must always be loosely attached to its backing with hinges. These hinges should not be Scotch tape or masking tape. Instead, use (or ask for) a tough-fibered Japanese paper hinge. It should not be thicker or stronger than the paper of the print itself.

5. Be sure that mat and backboard are properly connected with gummed white linen tape.

6. Commercial pastes or glues may stain. A homemade natural paste of rice starch and water is much better for attaching hinges to paper, also for repositioning a silhouette if one unluckily comes loose from its mounting.

7. Ask for three or more hinges at the top of a large print; two are usually enough for smaller prints.

8. A mat opening is more attractive if there is slightly more margin of mat at the bottom than at the top.

9. The mat opening should leave some margin of a print to show through—especially if a signature or other information appears there.

FRAMING

It is most important that glass does not directly touch the paper. There is always a possibility that condensation will cause moisture to form. If there is no mat—perhaps for aesthetic or historic reasons—a rag board strip should be inserted between glass and print where it won't show under the frame. Never frame prints pressed between two sheets of glass.

Routine Care

There is no routine care of art on paper other than protection. Cleaning a print with day-old bread or an art gum eraser sounds simple, but isn't. Held the wrong way, either can rip a print. "Also," explains Mrs. Gaehde, "a nonprofessional would only be able to clean the margins, leaving the signature or other areas soiled and the effect worst than before."

Frames should be sealed to keep out dust, which eliminates that aspect of housekeeping. Unframed prints should be kept in protective matting and if they are in a collection that will be handled from time to time, glassine or mylar sheets can be loosely inserted to shield the face of the print.

Special Problems

RIPS   Never try to mend a print yourself if it is of any value at all. The best course of action is to place it between two clean, smooth pieces of cardboard and take it to a restorer. For art on paper whose only worth is a sentimenal one, use masking tape (never cellophane tape, which bends and discolors as it ages) to hold the tear together across the back.

WARPING OR BUCKLING   As atmospheric conditions change, paper may expand and contract, developing "waves." Make no effort to correct this, as stretching, dry-mounting, pasting, or attempting to iron flat all lead to results worse than the original trouble. Paper will probably return to normal with time and maintenance of even temperature and humidity.

FLY SPECKS AND OTHER SPOTS   Removing these or any stains from paper is, again, a job for experts. Sometimes a spot can be taken off by barely dampening it with hydrogen peroxide on a Q-Tip, immediately wiping off with another Q-Tip and distilled water, then immediately blotting dry. However, this runs a risk. A glaring white spot may be the result, and as Mrs. Gaehde points out, "Often a conservator finds it impossible to repair the damage when an amateur has tried to clean paper and failed."

Do's and Don'ts for Prints, Pastels, and Watercolors

DO maintain an even temperature and humidity for all art on paper; air should preferably circulate behind the picture, too.

DON'T hang in sunlight or other strong light.

DO replace old backing and soiled mats with museum-quality 100 percent rag board.

DON'T try do-it-yourself cleaning methods.

DO be sure that instead of commercial glues, a homemade paste of rice starch and water is used.

DON'T allow glass to touch the face of the paper.

DO ignore paper rippling from atmospheric changes, treating this by controlling temperature and humidity rather than by direct methods.

DON'T attempt to repair valuable prints yourself.

MIRRORS, REVERSE PAINTINGS, AND
TRANSFER PRINTS ON GLASS

All the rules for preventing accidents to your pictures—checking screws, hanging hooks, and so forth—apply doubly to this category. Shatter the glass and a reverse painting or transfer print will be lost entirely; break an antique looking glass and a good deal of the value is lost, even when the frame is its major attraction. (If, incidentally, you must *use* an antique mirror for reflection and want to replace the wavy or cloudy glass, have the old glass put carefully away in a safe place in case you ever want to sell it, since the original glass increases its worth.) Some of the early mirrors, made at a time when silvered glass was precious and rare, may be in two parts, and any collector knows better than to think this is a flaw.

After avoiding breakage, the next most important concern with this category is to keep the coating on the back from peeling. It is quite difficult for a conservator to restore a damaged transfer print or reverse painting on glass (besides, the expense involved would rarely be proportionate to the value) and old mirrors are never the same when resilvered. Temperature and humidity control, those faithful allies of the antiques lover, will help prevent peeling to some degree. Never spray-clean the front of the glass, since liquid might seep through inside. Instead, use a lint-free cloth (an old diaper is good) dampened with water and ammonia or Windex to wipe glass clean, then polish dry.

If there still seems to be some tendency to peel, check the backing. Sometimes old backing material encourages moisture to form. Carefully remove it, working slowly and with caution to be sure nothing is stuck to the glass (in which case only a professional can get it off safely). Then cut a piece of white, acid-free blotting paper (available in art stores) to exact size and press gently against the back of the glass. This should help hold any fragments in place. Needless to say, you should never paste or glue this or any other backing to the glass; glues often eat through the very medium you want to preserve.

SAMPLERS AND THEOREM PAINTINGS

Even if old paper backing looks intact and unstained, it is particularly important to replace it behind framed samplers, painted velvet, or other antique fabrics under glass. Insects as well as dirt may be harbored there to work their way to the front. Old wood as a backing may lead to stains. Ask a framer if he will put in a backing sheet treated with moth and silverfish preventive, but don't try to handle these toxic substances yourself. Don't forget that samplers and theorems should also never be framed in direct contact with their glass.

Other precautions for hanging objects in this chapter are equally relevant when applied to framed textiles. Strong sunlight in particular is damaging to fabrics, and will not only fade but weaken them.

DAGUERREOTYPES

The first practical technique for achieving a photographic likeness was patented in 1839 by the Frenchman Daguerre. *Daguerreotypes* were made on a copper plate with a silver-fused surface and light-sensitive emulsion. Very similar to an untutored eye are two later techniques, the *ambrotype* and the *tintype,* both of which were developed around 1851. All three versions were immensely popular by the time of the Civil War, as we can see by the many pictures of sad-eyed soldiers and their loved ones dating from the period of that conflict.

Because treatment differs for each, it is important to identify which you have, according to Robert Sobieszek, Assistant Curator in Research, International Museum of Photography, Rochester, New York. It is not difficult to distinguish among the three. Daguerreotypes have a mirrorlike surface and usually must be tilted slightly to show the image. Ambrotypes, on the other hand, can be seen directly and easily, since they were made on glass rather than a metal plate. A tintype (which is not on tin at all, but on thin sheet iron) appears flatter in both color and tone, lacking the depth shown by the ambrotype.

A daguerreotype is extremely delicate; it is usually covered with glass because the image is no thicker than smoke and can be removed with a whisk of a camel's-hair brush. Obviously, you must not dust or wash the surface of a daguerreotype. Without the protection of glass, it shouldn't be handled at all. If an old daguerreotype is hard to see and seems dirty, the only recommended cleaning approach is to remove the glass—with great care—and either wash the glass or replace it with new. Sometimes old glass is irredeemably pitted or cloudly, and replacement is the best answer. Apparently daguerreotypes are not yet "antique" enough for the old glass to be considered essential to the value. If you decide to clean the glass, don't use ammonia-type cleaners such as Windex—ammonia fumes can fade the image. To repeat, *never* wash the daguerreotype itself.

An ambrotype is somewhat sturdier than a daguerreotype, but you should examine it closely to see whether the image is on top of the glass, on the back of the glass, or sandwiched between two pieces of glass. You can use a damp cloth to wipe off the protected surface of an ambrotype, but not the image itself. Often an ambrotype is coated with black lacquer on the reverse. If this layer comes off, you will temporarily lose some of the image due to lack of dark contrast. Safer than repainting it is to put a backing of good black velvet in its place. (*Don't glue* velvet against the ambrotype; glues or pastes will eat through the image.) The image returns as if by magic with the replacement of the contrasting dark backing.

The so-called tintype is the least delicate of the three and can even be washed directly. Use distilled water to avoid any unfortunate chemical reaction; don't soak; and instead of rubbing dry with a cloth, simply let circulating warm air dry your tintype quickly. Washing is not, of course, to be considered a routine procedure. It is done only if the tintype is badly soiled. Presumably it won't have to be repeated.

General Precautions

Strong light fades all varieties of photographs, so be careful not to hang them in sunlight. Exposure to air (and the usual industrial pollutants) can also be harmful, and ideally a collection should be housed under glass. To fit a frame more snugly to the picture, never paste or glue; instead use bits of 100 percent rag museum-quality board to fill in spaces. The frames and ornately decorated cases, sometimes made of leather, gutta-percha, or the earliest commercial plastic, are worthy of special care, too. Treat leather according to instructions in Chapter 7 (see under books). Wash plastic or gutta-percha carefully with lukewarm distilled water. And never allow yourself to be so carried away with the beauties of the cases—as some collectors have been in the past—that you discard the fragment of individual history represented by the likeness.

7

PERSONAL CARE FOR
SPECIAL COLLECTIONS

GUNS

THE way to a man's heart is definitely *not* through cleaning his gun collection. Even more than throwing out his old hunting clothes (and any hunter's wife knows what a trauma that would be), touching a man's antique guns is the first step toward the divorce court.

Those who collect firearms usually become very knowledgeable about their care. Damage in cleaning is more often done by an overenthusiastic wife or a household helper, so carried away with television's white knight that she scrubs a gun with kitchen abrasives (unbelievable as this sounds, it is a factual report by a curator who told me of having seen the results of such misguided helpfulness). Water alone is almost as destructive a cleaning agent, since it encourages the major hazard to firearms: rust.

A true gun collector, according to an armorer who cares for an important museum collection, will go to great lengths to protect his collection from moisture. He may even insist that anybody handling the guns first don cotton gloves. This is actually a wise precaution; fingerprints, especially in the summer, soon turn to rust. The collection should be kept in a stable atmosphere of low temperature and relative humidity, though not so low that excessive dryness causes wooden stocks to split.

Methods of cleaning a firearm vary; what would be good for metal with a blue finish might be bad for one with a brown finish. Oue curator of arms advises taking the mildest approach, using caution. For instance, an emery cloth is safe *only* in expert hands. A nonprofessional may find that it removes color and scratches the surface. Instead, it is safer to clean the exterior metal of a gun with 0000 steel wool and kerosene. Flush off the kerosene with wood alcohol, polish dry, and finish with a thin coating of paste wax. Before using any wax, check the label carefully to be sure it isn't water based and has no tannic acid (litmus paper is a test, if you want to double-check). Wooden stocks should be waxed too. Their care would follow guidelines in this book's chapter on wooden furniture. As for the working parts of a gun, each collector usually has his own favorite oil, suitable for gun and reel, from a good sporting supplies store.

It is important to keep a gun collection well dusted (wearing those cotton gloves, of course) because dust attracts moisture, and moisture, rust.

MECHANICAL BANKS

These brightly painted, cast-iron tributes to the thrift ethic are attracting collectors today as they did children's pennies in their heyday. Although mechanical banks and similar metal toys are rarely over a hundred years old (they can be dated with some accuracy through patent listings in Washington, D. C.), enough collections have been formed to push the prices of choice items well up into the scale of antiques. According to Mrs. Ashely Giles, buyer of Antique Toys for F. A. O. Schwartz, the toys without much action tend to be rare and therefore more valuable. "The most expensive ones are not as likely to be complicated—the reason they were not popular and produced in quantity in their day —or else they are too complicated."

Preserving the value of old mechanical banks and toys depends largely on leaving them alone. "More toys are ruined by attempting to clean and restore them than by anything else," John Noble, Curator of the Toy Collection, the Museum of the City of New York, says. Mrs. Giles agrees: "The minute you use paint on a toy, you devalue it."

Your objective should be to disturb and handle your toys as little as possible. Never repaint under any circumstances. The only approved treatment is one that halts further deterioration. Since paint has often worn off, leaving the cast iron or tin unshielded, a thin coat of wax will substitute as a protective coating. Mrs. Giles suggests using a liquid cleaning wax to remove dirt from a newly acquired toy, avoiding abrasives whenever possible. Just wax once—periodic rewaxing would rarely be desirable. Dust, when necessary, with a feather duster and a gentle touch.

Mechanical banks and toys that command a good price are expected to work. You can use a little light machine oil to keep moving parts in operation, but don't be tempted to tinker. Cast iron is difficult to solder, and to be acceptable, repairs must be made with old parts. Specialists use bits and pieces saved from incomplete antique banks or toys. Consult an expert, if you can, for guidance on repairs.

DOLLS

Dolls, perhaps more than any other antique, are wrapped in an aura of nostalgia. Thoughts of the little girls who treasured them in years gone by, or of colonial ladies eagerly noting details from a new French fashion doll surround such collections with sentiment.

"If only," says John Noble of the Museum of the City of New York, "more collectors would realize that their dolls are a less vivid link with the past if restored. Instead of making replacements, they should adjust to the idea of imperfection. Collectors of Greek bronzes or Roman sculptures don't worry if fragments are missing."

The prime rule for the care of dolls is to preserve them as they are, rather than trying to restore them to their original perfection. Never repaint. "In general," Mr. Noble continues, "it is better to have a doll that is dingy or incomplete rather than risk ruining it by overenthusiastic cleaning." He points to the possibility that paint may easily be scrubbed off a doll's face (although color is fired on a china doll, it is often not well fired, and papier-mâché dolls are painted with something like watercolors). Chlorine bleaches are also likely to be damaging, and many French lady dolls have permament marks on their cheeks where abrasives were tried. Mr. Noble himself never uses anything stronger than a very mild baby soap (Pears transparent) to wash china or bisque faces, if dirty, and even this treatment should be attempted with care.

Washing a doll's clothes is, if anything, more hazardous than washing its face. Sulphur dioxide is a common air pollutant that may be clinging to a dress; put the dress in water and sulphuric acid is created, leaving the dress in shreds.

"Obviously, you must use your intelligence to judge carefully each case," Mr. Noble believes. He does approve the kind of restoration designed to preserve. For instance, something should be done when a dress is covered with oily soot or mold or when clothes are pinned to the doll body with rusty pins (but if an 1830 doll has handmade pins of the same period, leave them).

If you are unhappy with a doll's dress, don't try to fix it. Just put it carefully aside (marking it so that someone else can tell which doll it belongs to) and make an entirely new dress, consulting museums and encyclopedias for period styles and using old materials and trim if possible.

Dolls will thrive in an atmosphere of stable temperature and relative humidity. They should not be subjected to bright, blazing lights, whether natural or artificial. Incandescent lights are too hot, fluorescent lights cause chemical reactions, sunlight causes fading. Serious collectors try to display their dolls in rooms that will be dimly lit; when stored, dolls are usually kept in boxes (never in plastic bags, which encourage moisture through condensation).

BOOKS AND OTHER ITEMS OF LEATHER AND PAPER

Although a bibliophile, like everyone else, is interested in the content of his books, he must save a major portion of concern for the bindings and pages. In truth, the material that encloses a book is apt to be far more perishable than its ideas. Mold and mildew lie in wait for the paper; untended leather bindings can become powdery and crumble; and there really is a bookworm to guard against.

To simplify guidelines for the proper care of books, they are divided under three headings: *books* as entities (general hints on maintaining a library), *leather* bindings (care that can be applied to other leather objects), and *paper* pages.

Books

The proper treatment for an antique book parallels that of any other book—only more so. Never "crack" books open against their bindings. Never turn down a corner or use a thick bookmark to keep your place. Don't stand books lengthwise on edge with the spine up.

On shelves, volumes should be stacked close enough together so they do not fall or lean, but with space for air to circulate. An exception to this general rule is made for books bound in vellum, which should be placed tightly together so they won't fluff out. Frequent examination, brushing, and airing are important to guard books against damage from insects and bookworm (actually an insect larva that chews both bindings and pages). These precautions are especially necessary in warm, humid climates.

Maintaining an even temperature and relative humidity is particularly important for books. Spines split when old volumes are brought from a damp climate to a dry, steam-heated apartment. Excess humidity, on the other hand, encourages both insects and mold.

Of all the hazards to books, by far the most dangerous is the human one. Curators urge that collectors *never* attempt repairs on their own. Minor damage becomes irretrievable ruin after an amateur tries to fix it. Mending a book, whether binding or leaves, requires an expert, who often uses tools and techniques little changed since the Middle Ages. Many rare-book dealers refuse to consider the purchase of any book that has been taped or pasted in any way by an amateur, who with the best of intention sadly destroys the value of his treasures.

Leather

Caring for leather is primarily a matter of preventing trouble; once leather has become powdery, hardened, or bacteria invaded, very little can be done. If you really care about bindings or other objects of leather, you would be well advised to install air conditioning and proper humidfying equipment as safeguards. Atmospheric pollutants lead to the irreversible powdering of leather, and although potassium lactate in a dressing (see Chapter 10) helps protect against this, clean air is better still. Dressings may temporarily improve the appearance of powdery leather, experts will sometimes "reconstitute" it (which alters the looks), but nothing can return it to the original condition.

Extreme heat or dampness will harden leather, and both are obviously to be avoided. If leather has unintentionally been thoroughly hardened (some leather objects, such as fire buckets, were meant to be hard), there is nothing you can do to make it supple again, and attempts may do still more damage by cracking or breaking the leather. If, however, leather is in basically sound but stiffened condition, you can usually bring it back with lubrication. (*Do not attempt to lubricate parchment, vellum or rawhide.* Rawhide is untanned, lasts in dry climates, but in constant dampness it will putrefy quickly. Vellum and parchment are already oily by nature.) Experts differ on the best approach. Some use saddle soap and/or commercial emulsions. Others swear by neat's-foot oil or castor oil (though many feel that these are too messy for book bindings).

When applying dressings to maintain leather in good condition (this should be done routinely once or twice a year), use as little as possible and rub in with your hands; friction and warmth will aid penetration. If you are treating books, a sensible idea is to protect paper from oily stains by inserting a piece of wax paper between binding and fly leaf. Always work carefully around gold-leaf lettering or decoration—a water-based preparation may lift the leaf.

Stains can be very difficult to remove from leather; avoiding them is the best policy. However, if leather is soiled, brush or vacuum loose dirt away, then with a lint-free cloth apply saddle soap to spots, wiping off again. Mold and mildew shouldn't occur if you maintain a level relative humidity and adequate ventilation. Treatment consists of brushing, cleaning with saddle soap, and leaving the item in fresh air and sunshine for several hours.

Paper

The rules for paper conservation in Chapter 6 (under Prints, Pastels, and Watercolors) apply equally to pages of books or to collections of paper valentines.

It bears repeating that you must *never* mend a tear with cellophane tape of any variety. This is undoubtedly the single most serious cause of unthinking damage, especially to books. The tape will harden, distorting the paper, and it is quite difficult to remove without further injury to the paper. Even when the tape is taken off, discoloration will usually remain. Fastening loose pages back into an old book, unless professionally done, lowers the value. You should, in fact, make it a firm rule never to attempt any sort of resoration of paper.

Documents, maps, or any papers that you care about should not be attached to cardboard. This leads to staining and other deterioration. Instead, use 100 percent rag board and follow mounting instructions in Chapter 6. To protect individual papers, such as old letters, place them loosely inside clear plastic envelopes (these are available to fit in loose-leaf notebooks, a good idea if you have a group of papers to preserve). Don't seal them.

You can look at a morning newspaper left for a day in the sun for quick evidence of the yellowing effects of sunlight on paper. Although results will be slower on better grades of paper, you should nonetheless be warned that strong sunlight is damaging. Paper should also be protected from excess humidity (which leads to mildew and mold) and from extremes of temperature.

CLOCKS

The tall, handsome, grandfather clock and its petite relation, the grandmother (usually four feet tall rather than seven or eight feet), are often thought of primarily as furniture. Their wooden cases are beautiful additions to a room and should be given the same care described in Chapter 2 for fine cabinetwork. Mantel and shelf clocks may also be of wood and be treated similarly. But clock cases were made in a wide range of materials, particularly after the Willards patented their idea for a banjo clock in the early 1800's. You may find clocks of brass, bronze, cast iron, alabaster, and silver, so look through the appropriate chapters to find out how to treat the case of your own timepiece. For alabaster, follow the guidelines for marble, Chapter 2.

Many clocks have painted glass panels (reverse paintings);

these should not be cleaned directly and certainly never varnished. To keep the paint from flaking, cut a piece of white acid-free blotting papper (from an art store) and carefully wedge it against the back of the painting to prevent further peeling (never use glue to attach the blotter).

Clocks are a unique combination of the decorative and the useful, and the condition of their works is as important as the condition of their exteriors. Repairing the working parts of a clock requires an expert, so if you own a valuable clock, you should be sure that nobody tinkers with it except a specialist. Both the Horological Institute of America and the American Institute of Watch Repairing award certificates of proficiency. The National Association of Watch and Clock Collectors, Box 33, Columbia, Pennsylvania 17512, which publishes an informational bulletin, may also be able to provide guidance in finding someone qualified to deal with antique clockworks. It is a good idea to have your clock cleaned and oiled every five to ten years. If you are buying an old clock with plans to have it put in running order, you should realize that major repairs will not be inexpensive.

Assuming that you own a working timepiece, there are a few general rules to keep in mind:

1. Wind your clock regularly, preferably at the same time— each day for a "thirty-hour" clock, each week for an "eight-day" clock.

2. When winding a spring-powered clock, be sure that the key fits securely and do not release it suddenly.

3. The pendulum is not, as many people think, a source of power, but its indication or "escapement." Nevertheless, it is an important and delicate part of the clock's mechanism. The pendulum's suspension spring determines the rate of time the clock keeps, so be careful not to bend it. If you are moving a clock a

short way, tilt it backward so the pendulum is supported by the back of the case. For a major move, it is safer to take the pendulum out entirely.

4. Choose a location for your clock that is away from direct heat, which will dry out both the case and the lubricating oil in the mechanism. Also try to avoid a location such as a passageway where your clock will be subjected to jars from people going by.

5. Keeping your clock in perfect beat depends upon its being positioned in exact balance. Listen to the sound and move the bottom of a wall clock either to left or right until ticking is perfectly even. (Mark the position on the wall with pencil so the clock can be easily repositioned after dusting.) A tall clock or shelf clock may need a thin piece of cardboard or wood under the front, back, or side to level it. If you have trouble with this, call in a professional.

6. Don't try to clean the clock mechanism yourself. The inside of the case, however, should be dusted from time to time. Use the small brush of your vacuum turned to low suction, rather than flicking a cloth, which might scatter dust into the moving parts. Carefully check first to be sure there are no old paper labels that will come loose. Such labels or any other indication of the maker's name add immeasurably to the value of your clock, and experts deplore the sort of overenthusiastic scrubbing that might obscure them.

7. It is not a good idea to move clock hands backward. It will damage some clocks, and it often takes an expert to tell which ones.

DECOYS

The decoy, rarely found in other countries, is a peculiarly American device for luring birds from the air. It can't be claimed as a product of Yankee ingenuity, because Indians were producing and setting out decoys (made of rushes or birds' skins) as early as A.D. 1000. Undoubtedly the great clouds of waterfowl that moved in migratory patterns across this country in its early years (sadly decimated since by hunters) were the inspiration for the creation of decoys. And the talent and skill of the men who whittled and painted shore birds and marsh fowl have made their work a genuine category of American folk art.

As collectibles, decoys actually belong in two categories: those intended for use—shore birds that perch above the sand on sticks, or floating ducks and geese—and decorative birds that were never meant to go out in the wind and weather. Their care from a housekeeping standpoint varies accordingly. Although wax is advised for almost every other wooden antique, it should not be used on working decoys because it would detract from their authenticity. A polished, gleaming wooden bird would have reflected light and warned off the flocks flying overhead, so that is not the appearance you want today.

Decorative birds, however, were considered pieces of art in their own time, and a thin coating of paste wax (see Chapter 2 for care of wood) is excellent as a preservative, and does not detract from the validity of the surface. The better carvers used well-seasoned wood, but since most decoys spent a large portion of their lives immersed in water, cracking of the wood can be a problem. Control of relative humidity is a major key, but in addition, you may want to use a bit of oil. Linseed oil will eventually dry to a hard surface, so it is better to use a pure, nondrying oil (perhaps lemon oil) dropped into large crevices and rubbed into the surface, then thoroughly wiped off.

Above all, don't try to put your decoys back in their original condition. Adele Earnest, co-owner of the Stony Point Folk Art Gallery and author of the definitive book on decoys, *The Art of the Decoy*, states firmly, "Any repainting lowers the value." She goes on to add, "I feel the only legitimate reason for touching up is when a decoy-maker is so well known for paint patterns—and traces which remain can be *restored*. But paints are different now, and I myself have nothing that is either repainted or restored."

Very few decoys were unpainted. As a rule they were sealed with white lead paint (though scorching the outside was a method for sealing too), then decorated with appropriate markings in a variety of ways. Makers brushed, stippled, and sometimes even combed the final coat of paint.

The decoy as an art form has continued up to the present. Some of the most important carvers are still alive, although the most desirable birds from a collector's standpoint date prior to 1920. Still, it is one of the few antique categories with a sense of continuity into the present day and into every area of the country where the nostalgic sound of migrant birds calling marks the seasons.

SCRIMSHAW AND OTHER IVORY

The scratching of decorations on ivory is said to go back to the Phoenicians, but what collectors (among them President John F. Kennedy) call scrimshaw was produced by American seamen, primarily during the great whaling era. Far more men were carried on whaling ships than were needed to operate them; the pattern was a few days of furious activity requiring every man on board, followed by long days of calm cruising, when men had idle time to fill, and filled it by decorating the ivory that was so handy.

It is encouraging to collectors to be assured by Revell Carr, Curator of Mystic Seaport, that "ivory is a fairly stable material." According to Mr. Carr, scrimshaw does well with a great deal of leaving alone. The only cleaning recommended is an occasional dusting with a soft, lint-free cloth. "Never wash scrimshaw," Mr. Carr advises, "since the dyes in the decoration might come off. There is no knowing what was used. It might have been tobacco juice, India ink, soot, anything easily available on shipboard. If you have acquired a piece of scrimshaw that is badly soiled, take it to a professional conservator for cleaning rather than risk a loss of the engraving."

The greatest hazard to scrimshaw, as to other small antique items, is excessive handling or dropping. If you can, find a display area out of temptation's way, where children or neighbors won't touch.

When ivory ages, it often becomes yellowed, which is considered a natural and attractive patina. Don't try to bleach it, even if the discoloring is uneven; this would damage both the appearance and value. For the same reason, if there are stains, ignore them. Ivory (other than scrimshaw) can be washed, although of course you must use good judgment. A priceless piece of oriental carving, for instance, should only be entrusted to a professional. The major precaution in cleaning ivory is to minimize the amount of time it is in contact with water. Water can soften ivory, cause layers to separate, and eventually cause decomposition. Obviously, to prevent water from penetrating, you should work quickly—and when ivory is cracked or the surface otherwise deteriorated, don't wash it at all. Wiping with a damp, lint-free cloth, followed by immediate drying, is safest. If this does not remove soot or grease, try a cloth dampened with alcohol. To clean really heavy dirt (from a not very valuable piece) use a mild soap and water solution, scrub quickly (with a brush, since the faster the cleaning, the less chance of damage), wipe off with a damp cloth, and dry.

Ivory is a relatively sturdy material, but it, too, benefits from an environment of stable relative humidity and temperature. Heat and damp will easily warp it. Never leave a piece of valuable ivory in direct sunlight, which will bleach it. On the other hand and for the same reason, to keep instrument keys from excessive yellowing, don't close away the keyboard.

8 HOUSEKEEPING WHEN OUR ANTIQUES WERE YOUNG

Addres to all

"Ladis, How lightly soever men esteem those Feminine Arts of Government which are practiced in the Regulation of an Household, I may venture to Assert, they are of much more intrinsick value than some admired branches of literature, for to say the truth, what can be really of greater Use than by Prudence and Good Management to supply a Family with all things that are convenient, from a Fortune, which without such care could scarce afford Necessaries? Certainly no Art Whatsoever relating to terrestial things, ought to claim a preference to that which makes Life easy."

The Housekeeper's Pocket Book
London, 1733

ALTHOUGH housekeeping is rarely mentioned when lists of "the oldest professions" are compiled, it is ignored more from lack of professional status than from lack of age. Isn't it likely that the first cave woman used a few twigs to sweep out old dinosaur bones? Certainly by biblical times Martha was a familiar prototype of the superhousekeeper.

125

Fleeting glimpses of the household arts appear here and there during the next centuries, but it wasn't until the full burst of Renaissance life that serious attention began to be paid to the pleasures of a properly furnished and attended home.

Even then, interest in a well-regulated house was a distinctly hit or miss affair. Travelers to Italy commented on the great contrasts—in a single household—between luxury and squalor. A bed would be covered in silk, while overhead a ceiling of reeds revealed the roof tiles. The walls of a palace might be hung with masterpieces, while dogs and geese quarreled over bones beneath the dinner table. At that, Italian households during the Renaissance were in a far more civilized state than those of other European countries, and the earliest impulses toward the decorative arts usually originated in Italy.

In England, the Elizabethans were beginning to be grandly (if uncomfortably) seated upon heavily wainscoted, thronelike chairs. Their ideas of housekeeping were correspondingly stronger on show than on substance.

While the thought of a moated castle complete with knights and fair ladies waving from crenelated towers has a fetchingly romantic sound, reality was something else. A contemporary account urged that "moats should be fresh, cleaned frequently and not used as a dump for kitchen waste and worse," with the strong implication that all but the uncommon moats resembled sewers. If we stop to think of the total disinterest in formal bathroom arrangements shared by our robust antecedents, it is no wonder their moats might not have invited close inspection. A godson of Queen Elizabeth invented the water closet during her reign, but with typical British disdain for plumbing, it was almost two centuries before it was perfected and in accepted use.

Of course towers with moats and their accompanying upkeep

problems belonged to the relative few, but interiors and house-keeping attitudes varied only in size and elaboration from castle down to wattle-and-daub hut. Dusting was a minimal activity, since furniture was scanty in most homes throughout the sixteenth century and even into the seventeenth. (Remember all those wills delegating the great chair or second-best bed?) Chairs were originally only for V.I.P.'s. Their elaborate, heavy carving fit them for ecclesiastics or royalty, and as their use increased, they were still reserved for the head of the house or honored guests, while wives and other lesser mortals managed with benches or stools. "Chairman of the board" in those days was a perfectly literal term for the husband who sat at the head of a table, made usually of a large board set on trestles. Chests of drawers were beginning to evolve from the earlier storage chests, but by far the most important piece of furniture was the massive, room-dominating bed. It was enormous, elaborately carved, for-midably draped, and with curtains closed, a haven of warmth in drafty sixteenth-century rooms. It lacked, however, the simple modern comforts of bed springs and frequently changed sheets. The huge linen bed sheets were so difficult to launder and dry in damp weather that as a rule they weren't washed for months on end. They were too expensive to own in quantity, as we can guess from frequent records of borrowed "lying-in sheets" for childbirth. Since they couldn't be laundered, they couldn't be changed at all. And housewives were constantly exchanging recipes guaranteed (apparently in vain) to rid their bedsteads of "bugges."

If we'd rather not delve further into the conditions of sixteenth-century beds, let alone spend a night in one, still less would we enjoy a closer look at the floors our ancestors trod. The great hall, their principal room, served many functions, and the reeds covering its floor hid the remnants of a multiplicity of events. It was considered a sign of excellent housekeeping if fresh rushes were spread on the floor from time to time, but they were simply strewn on top, without removing what must have been unimaginable debris beneath. Meals for the entire company were served in this room, and morsels or bones often dropped down to nestle in the rushes after being gnawed by the ever-present hounds. Even when lavender, rosemary, and other sweet-smelling herbs were added to the floor reeds, it is still not hard to imagine why both men and women of the time were so fond of strong perfumes.

Added to the pungent aroma inside houses was a good deal of smoke from the large open fires used for cooking and heat. In early days and in poor homes, a hole in the ceiling was the only outlet for this smoke. Toward the end of Queen Elizabeth's reign, when mantels and chimneys were being used with increasing efficiency in England, it is amusing to read the dire warnings from the older generation. These elders were convinced that just as smoke toughened the timber of the houses, it also toughened the physical strength (and perhaps the character) of the inmates, so they predicted an immediate weakening of the fiber of the nation's younger, unsmoked generation.

Other refinements were being introduced in the wake of the great wealth spreading to Europe from New World silver mines. Wooden utensils were being replaced by pewter for the average man, silver or gold plate for the upper classes. Spoons were coming into more common use, although they were still special enough to be given to babies as a choice christening present (hence our "born with a silver spoon in his mouth"). Forks were introduced as an exotic import from Italy. This increasing amount of household silver was usually cleaned by boiling with such vigor it is surprising any survived at all.

If the sixteenth-century housekeeping approach seems coarse and unappetizing in many ways, on the reverse side these houses were filled with color and vitality. Vivid shades—scarlets, violets, the brightest hues—were favorites and appeared in clothes, painted panelings, mullioned window panes, as well as the tapestries used both to decorate and warm the cold walls. And to give credit to a burgeoning interest in cleanliness, we should mention an admirable if drastic total housecleaning technique. When one house reached the disgracefully dirty stage, its mistress simply packed up family and retinue and moved to another, leaving instructions behind for top to bottom cleaning—even throwing out those accumulated floor rushes. This was fondly referred to as "sweetening," and must surely have been a reason (if only a minor one) for such constant traveling over deplorable roads. Then, as now, it is a variety of housekeeping limited to those rich enough to own several houses, but it had the merit of simplicity. Its echo is still around today when a housewife says she likes to move periodically, if only to clean out the closets.

The seventeenth century brought in some welcome household innovations. Straw matting came into fashion as a floor covering to replace strewn rushes, and was considerably easier to keep clean. Turkey carpets were still used primarily as furniture covers, but by the late 1600's they were being tried on floors. Puritan influence may have encouraged simple styles in furniture (perhaps because of our Pilgrim beginnings, furniture in the New World was always a less elaborate version of European styles). And very gradually, homes were filling up with lighter and more comfortable pieces (new inventions like the winged chair, for instance). Furniture was still somewhat hard and stiff-looking to modern eyes, though, and it is difficult to picture angular Jacobean or even Queen Anne styles as fitting Shakespeare's earlier description of a "lewd daybed."

Along with convenience, luxury was increasing. Not even Cromwell's rule could entirely stop the nouveau riche instinct to show off wealth, and with the Restoration, it burst forth with renewed vigor. In France the eighteenth century brought forth perhaps the most gorgeous preoccupation with the decorative arts the world has ever seen. Beginning with the guidance of Louis XIV, generations of noble families beggared the next so repeatedly that a duke commented in 1770: "It is the cost of their houses which has crushed most of the great families." Every detail was refined: chamber pots were made in chiseled silver and soft paste porcelain; gaming became a passion and produced delicate boxes inlaid with ivory and mother-of-pearl to hold the counters; small bedroom kennels for dogs were handsomely molded, carved, painted, and gilded; even science became decorative with microscopes and mathematical instruments decorated by the ébénistes. Attitudes toward housekeeping were similarly aristocratic, typified by Madame de Pompadour who constantly sent pieces of furniture back to Lazare Duvaux to have the gilt-bronze mounts cleaned.

It was left to the more middle-class English to display silver plate as evidence of advanced status, then to write domestic guides on how to polish it. Samuel Pepys and others might look around a new "dining room" with self-satisfied pleasure at the surrounding gleam of silver plate, but coal fires and industrial soot called for more polishing than ever. The favorite method was still a vigorous "boyling," sometimes with Sal Ammoniac, Alum, Sal Gem, Tartar, and Roman Vitriol added to the water. It seems incredible that such treatment didn't simply dissolve the silver, and it is nice to know that a new and gentler approach was coming into vogue: polishing with a woolen cloth and a paste of wheat straw ashes, whiting, and burned alum.

We can admire the intent of other household cleaning recipes, while finding the methods less than appealing. To wipe off paint work of any kind, vine ashes mixed with fresh urine was recommended. It took from one to two weeks to clean discolored tablecloths with daily treatment ranging from a preliminary soaking in soft water and sheep dung, through applications of Dog's Mercury and strong boiling hot lye. No wonder used napkins were often just "pressed" and used again.

Such violent mixtures for cleaning house are less surprising when we consider what our ancestors put on their faces. Cosmetics, like medicines, were largely home brewed, and one favorite skin cleanser was based on oil of vitriol. Another beautifier called for powdered white mercury mixed with crushed egg shells, lemon juice, and white wine. White lead was a popular, if deadly, route to a fashionably pale complexion, and for rouge, such skin-eating dyes as red crystalline mercuric sulphide were much used.

If they wanted to be beautiful, why didn't they just bathe, we might wonder from our modern vantage point. For centuries personal cleanliness was even more haphazard than house cleaning. Queen Elizabeth was greatly admired for taking a bath once a month "whether she needed it or not"—understandable approval if it was true that James I was "as adverse to bathing as to naked steel." Even as late as the eighteenth century, there was a Duke of Norfolk who "could only be washed when he was dead drunk." If the upper and middle classes were disinterested in soap and water, the poor managed to avoid it almost entirely. The first gradual improvement in cleanliness for the lower classes began with the introduction of cotton clothing, which was inexpensive enough to change at intervals and could be washed if the owner desired. Before that, leather or woolen garments were worn through a lifetime, acquiring layers of filth along the way.

During the eighteenth century, that vintage period for chairs and statesmen, faint glimmerings of our modern interest in cleanliness began to appear. There were still tales of those who died from overbathing (John Williams, the satirist, was thought to have met death by washing his face), but most well-to-do homes had regular washings of household linen—called a bucking—three or four times a year. The upper classes stocked large quantities of linens, thirty-two tablecloths, for instance, in one noble house, which allowed reasonably frequent changes. And there was a surge of publications on the household arts which rose to a flood tide in the nineteenth century. They usually left out the recipes we'd most like to have today because "everybody knew them."

Volumes appeared under titles ranging from *Some rules and orders for the government of the house of an earle* to *Cottage Comforts*. There was *The British Housewife* (emanations of Imperial dignity) and *The Domestic Blunders of Women* "by a mere man" (pro- or anti-feminine?).

Some of these books were clearly produced by women with an inborn talent for housekeeping. Susanna Whatman is a good example. Her personal book of instructions for training new maids, written in 1776, is a delightful mixture of the quaint and the practical. And not a bad idea in itself. Though most of us today are lucky to have a cleaning lady, a written list of household do's and don'ts as a guide for help might save many a precious antique from harm. We may not have to remind anyone these days to keep candles upright to avoid dripping wax, but Mrs. Whatman's insistence that chairs or tables should be placed against a wall with a hand's space behind to avoid scarring is sensible. In the Whatman household, carpets and mats were to be shaken and curtains whisked weekly. A painter's brush was to be used to clean mahogany carvings, but nobody was to touch the pictures or girandoles (it was noted that Mrs. Whatman always cleaned these herself). An interesting custom of the day was to put large squares of heavy paper on top of the canopy of tester beds; these could then be removed easily and dusted. Another odd but ingenious idea was Mrs. Whatman's instruction to turn over all carpets to the wrong side when the family was away, "the intention of putting them so being that the walking on them should beat out the dust."

Other domestic manuals had less appealing suggestions. One urged readers to keep handy a flower pot with brick dust and damp hay or moss in which to plunge silver forks to clean them, which in time must have created an unappetizing mess. Juice of garlic was recommended to mend glass or china, and grated cheese mixed with quicklime to mend earthenware, surely two redolent solutions. Once a week was considered often enough to sweep bedrooms, first strewing used tea leaves on the floor. Ox gall mixed with powdered alum and common salt was used to clean carpets, and a favorite room freshener was a heated shovel with a teaspoon of coffee to burn where air was impure.

Chilton's One Thousand Secret Wrinkles favored strong spirits for cleaning almost everything, which gives us a pleasant picture of the homemaker gaily tippling through her day's duties. To sponge looking glasses? Spirits of wine rubbed rapidly over glass, followed by a dusting with sifted whiting, polished with an old silk handkerchief. To clean plate? Use whiskey and pulverized whiting. For heat marks on a table? First a hard rubbing with lamp oil, then a little spirits of wine.

Servants, of course, were a big item in all the period books on housekeeping. It is fascinating in our servantless era to read that housemaids should rise at 5 A.M. in the summer to have all fires made before 6 A.M. Household staff members were constantly exhorted to early rising, since, as one New York publication of 1834 explained, they could accomplish more in one hour before the family was up than in a full afternoon. Some early guides set a spirits allowance for servants; for example: "Ale—1 pint to the men and ½ a pint to the maids per day; small beer—as much as they chuse." Despite this, it was apparently never easy to get and keep efficient household help. Defoe approved of the man who married his cook/maid, "as then he would be always sure of a good dinner."

When the Victorian era settled heavily down over the world with a great draping of furbelows and swags, housekeeping guides turned their attention increasingly from recipes for cleaning to recipes for lengthy, many-course meals. Mrs. Beeton's famous book of household management was the best-selling model for all others, and her serious, all-encompassing advice went through multiple editions from the original in 1861 to a two-thousand-page tome in 1906. Any of these editions is intriguing to read today, with descriptions of such necessary household utensils as the digester, the hanging gridiron, the tongue presser, or the bread rasp.

Mrs. Beeton advises the mistress of the house to rise early (encouraging the servants to get up earlier still by her example) and to allow no servant on any account "to remain up after the heads of the house have retired." Everything from hand-sewing and counting the silver to morning calls is given equally weighty attention. Order and punctuality are urged, with a suggested printed card to regulate the times for household meals, prayers, and letter post. Recipes are given for soups to distribute to the poor (at a cost of one and a half pence per quart) or to serve dinner guests (a guinea per quart). Cleanliness was next to Godliness by now, according to the Victorian housekeepers, and a cold bath the only proper way to start each day.

By the latter part of the nineteenth century, the Industrial Revolution had shaped housekeeping into a mold not so terribly different from our modern routines, with commercial products replacing homemade ones, machines taking over from servants. Certainly homes and the world at large were more sanitary places. Less damage was done to furnishings, and households were far more orderly. But somehow, thinking back to the slightly soiled panache of the Elizabethans, there is a sense of loss—a reminder perhaps that housekeeping is not, as the Victorians seemed to view it, an end in itself. Rather, it is a necessary adjunct to the joys of living.

9 CURATORS' ADDRESS BOOK

(For Repairs, Replacement Parts, and Expert Service)

MEMBERS of museum and restoration staffs do most custodial work on their own collections. On occasions, however, they call in outside experts, such as those in the list that follows. These names have been supplied by curators, but there can of course be no guarantee of results in any individual case. This is another instance when your own good judgment and caution are required.

You may equally well locate other local craftsmen who can give careful and competent service to your antiques. Don't overlook the Fine Arts departments of local colleges or universities as a source of guidance. A number of museums, for instance, mentioned consulting Oberlin College about paintings. You may also inquire at your local museum, but you should realize that the conservation and curatorial staffs are often the busiest people in a museum, since each time an exhibition is mounted they have enormous responsibilities.

In writing to any of these experts for information, it would be wise to include a stamped, self-addressed envelope. And never fail to get an estimate in advance. Since these are trained and experienced specialists, they may charge accordingly.

137

ANTIQUE RUGS AND CARPETS, CLEANING OR REPAIRS

Avigdor's of Brookline
Brookline, Mass.

Bergmann's Rug Division
623 G. St. N. W.
Washington, D. C.

Blau, Vojtech
980 Madison Avenue
New York, N. Y.

Blazer Bros.
919 Main Street
Nashville, Tenn.

L. Condon Hooked Rugs, Cleaning-Repair Dept.
745 Burmont Road
Drexel Hill, Pa.

Mr. S. D. Derelian
800 Graham Hill Rd.
Santa Cruz, Calif.

Mr. Harry Kachadourian, Pres.
The Jamgotch Company
706 N. Howard Street
Baltimore, Md.   21201

Jerrebian Bros.
3731 Walnut St.
Philadelphia, Pa.

Kalamians Rug Shop, Inc.
963 Bank Street
New London, Conn.   06320

Mark Keshishian & Sons
  6930 Wisconsin Ave.
  Bethesda, Md.

Manoukian Bros., Inc.
  1862 Columbia Rd. N.W.
  Washington, D. C.   20009

K. A. Menendian, Inc.
  1090 West Fifth Ave.
  Columbus, Ohio   43212

Muradian Oriental Rug Co.
  2214-A Eliston Place
  Nashville, Tenn.

Musa Eid Musa
  1246 Perkiomen Ave.
  Reading, Pa.

Davis & H. Nahikian
  2108 Walnut St.
  Philadelphia, Pa.

Persia Rug Co., Mr. Ayoub
  Savannah, Ga.

Renofab Process Corporation (also cleans other textiles)
  755 East 134th Street
  Bronx, N. Y.   10454

James W. Rice Associates (also cleans other textiles)
  109 Lynnmoor Drive
  Silver Springs, Md.

Miss Verna Rowell (hooked rug repairs)
  605 S. Main Street
  West Franklin, N. H.

A. J. Skendarian
  La Salle Rd.
  West Hartford, Conn.

PAPER AND PRINTS, CONSERVATION

Mrs. Christa Gaehde
55 Falmouth Street
Arlington, Mass.   02174

Mrs. Mary Todd Glaser
73 East Linden Avenue
Englewood, N. J.   07631

Mr. William J. Hanft
The Brooklyn Museum
Brooklyn, New York   11238

Mrs. Marilyn Kemp
612 Spruce Street
Philadelphia, Pa.   19106

Mr. Harold W. Tribolet
R. R. Donnelley & Sons Co.
350 East 22nd Street
Chicago, Ill.   60616

Mr. John Washeba
79 Otis Street
Medford, Mass.

Mr. William Young
Head of the Research Laboratory
Boston Museum of Fine Arts
469 Huntington Ave.
Boston, Mass.   02115

OIL PAINTINGS, CLEANING

Julius Lowy, Inc. and Shar-sisto, Inc.
511 East 72nd Street
New York, N. Y.   10021

Renzo Baldaccini
    1100 Madison Ave.
    New York, N. Y.

Mr. Sandor Bodo
    Bodo's Art Studio
    6513 Highway 100
    Nashville, Tenn.   37205

Alain Boissonnas
    23 Bronson Ave.
    Scarsdale, N. Y.

Terence P. Bresnahan (paintings and prints)
    28 Glen Road
    Portsmouth, R. I.   02871

Mr. Chilton Powell
    Chilton's Fine Accessories For Interiors
    938-44 Conti Street
    Mobile, Ala.   36604

Roger W. Dennis, Conservator
    Lyman Allyn Museum
    100 Mohegan Ave.
    New London, Conn.   06320

Mr. and Mrs. Winston Dibble
    Shoreham, Vermont

Mrs. Dorothy Baden Elliott
    3655 Egerton Circle
    Sarasota, Fla.

Mr. S. J. Fishburne, Conservation of Paintings
    51 Old Ford Road
    New Paltz, N. Y.   12561

Mr. Victor E. Grace
Grace Galleries Inc.
Fine Arts Restorations
61 Grand Ave.
Englewood, N. J.   07631

Mr. Felrath Hines
54 West 74th Street
Studio #305
New York, N. Y.   10023

Hirschl & Adler Galleries
21 East 67th Street
New York, N. Y.

Mr. and Mrs. Sheldon Keck
Conservation of Historic and Artistic Works
Cooperstown Graduate Programs
Cooperstown, N. Y.   13326

Mr. Paul Kiehart
50 Crest Road
New Hyde Park, L.I., N. Y.

Mr. Gustav Klimann
561 Boyleston Street
Boston, Mass.   02116

Anton J. Konrad, Conservator of Sculpture
Conservation Laboratory
National Collection of Fine Arts and
National Portrait Gallery
Smithsonian Institution, Washington, D. C.   20560

Michael Melnitzky
1044 Madison Ave.
New York, N. Y.

Mr. Peter Michaels, Assoc. Conservator
    The Walters Gallery
    Baltimore, Md.   21201
    and
    Studio
    1922 South Road
    Baltimore, Md.   21209

Miss Elisabeth Packard, Director of Conservation
    The Walters Gallery
    Baltimore, Md.   21201

Mr. John Pogzeba
    600 South Emerson
    Denver, Colo.

Mr. Louis Pomerantz
    1424 Elinor Place
    Evanston, Ill.   60201

Mr. Bernard Rabin
    47 Halsey Street
    Newark, N. J.   07102

Mr. Clements L. Robertson
    City Art Museum of St. Louis
    St. Louis, Mo.   63105

Mr. Thornton Rockwell
    c/o The San Francisco Museum of Art
    McAllister at Van Ness
    San Francisco, Calif.   94102

Mr. James Roth, Resident Conservator
    William Rockhill Nelson Gallery of Art
    4525 Oak Street
    Kansas City, Missouri   64111

Mrs. Susanne P. Sack
    125 Remsen St.
    Brooklyn, N. Y.   11201

Miss Priscilla Sibley
Hillside Street
Scituate, Mass.

Miss Margot Sylvester
Hillside Street
Scituate, Mass.

Miss Jean Volkmer
The Museum of Modern Art
11 West 53rd Street
New York, N. Y.   10019

Miss Margaret Watherston
44 West 77th Street
New York, N. Y.   10024

Miss Tosca Zagni
The Museum of Modern Art
11 West 53rd Street
New York, N. Y.   10019

FURNITURE REPAIRS

Antiques and Restoration Center
231 East 77th Street
New York, N. Y.

Antique Furniture Restorers Corp.
225 East 24th Street
New York, N. Y.

Mr. Kenneth J. Covert (millwork reproductions—18th Century)
King's Highway
Fredericksburg, Va.

Mr. Caleb Davis (also upholstering)
c/o Dove & Distaff Antiques
Wakefield, R. I.

Charles Deacon
353 East 58th Street
New York, N. Y.

Mrs. Harry C. Hartmann
23 Lexington Ave.
Trenton, N. J.   08618

B. Lieberman & Son
16 South 20th Street
Philadelphia, Pa.

Oxford Antique Restorers Ltd.
37-20 48th Avenue
Long Island City, L. I., N. Y.

Mr. Robert Miller
Old Chatham, N. Y.   12136

P & W Cabinetmakers
312 East 95th Street
New York, N. Y.

Roman Arts Inc.
1801 First Avenue
New York, N. Y.

Herbert Schiffer
609 Lincoln Highway
Exton, Pa.   19341

Schneider & Son Antiques Inc.
175 E. 87th Street
New York, N. Y.

Charles Sundquist Inc.
319 East 53rd Street
New York, N. Y.

Thorp Bros.
410 East 62nd Street
New York City, N. Y.

Veleba and Hruban
27-11 24th Avenue
Astoria, Queens, N. Y.

John P. Western
Chatham Center, New York

REPRODUCTION OR PERIOD HARDWARE FITTINGS

Period Furniture Hardware Co.
(furniture brasses, wrought-iron fittings, and reverse paintings for mirrors and clocks)
123 Charles Street
Boston, Mass. 02114

Ball & Ball (stocks brass and wrought-iron reproductions; will also make special castings. Puts out brass polish called Glow which is used by some museums.)
463 West Lincoln Highway
Exton, Pa. 19341

CANING

Veterans Caning Shop
550 W. 35th Street
New York, N. Y. 10001

CERAMICS, REPAIRS

G. E. Caumont
(bric-a-brac repairs, vases mounted into lamps, etc.)
46 Christopher Street
Monclair, N. J. 07042

Harry A. Eberhardt & Son
2010 Walnut Street
Philadelphia, Pa. 19103

Hess Repairs (and glass repairs)
168 E. 33rd Street
New York City, N. Y.

F. Von Waldenburg
Cold Water Tavern Rd.
East Nassau, N. Y.   12062

Mrs. Dorothy Y. Wadsworth (also frames)
c/o Cohasset Historical Society
23 Cedar Lane
Cohasset, Mass.

GLASS, REPAIRS

Gem Monogram & Cut Glass Corp.
(liners for salts, bobeches, etc.)
623 Broadway
New York, N. Y.

White's Glass Co.
Race Street
Fredericksburg, Va.

CLOCKS

Mr. Francis M. Shirey
Gloucester, Va.

DRAPERY CLEANING

Neild
2205 N. Charles St.
Baltimore, Md.

Renofab Process Corporation (also cleans rugs)
755 East 134th Street
Bronx, N. Y.   10454

James W. Rice Associates (also cleans rugs)
109 Lynnmoor Drive
Silver Springs, Md.

CHANDELIERS AND WALLS, CLEANING

Hearn & Morrill & Co.
1201 Hunter Street
Baltimore, Md.   21202

METALS

Pewter, all metals

Michael J. Dotzel & Son, Expert Metal Craftsman
402 East 63rd Street
New York, N. Y.   10021
(lamps wired, mounted)

Silver, repairs

Simmons Silver Plating Co., Inc.
409 Whitehall St., S.W.
Atlanta, Ga.   30303

S. J. Shrubsole
104 E. 57th Street
New York, N. Y.

10 PRODUCTS FOR SAFE POLISHING AND CLEANING

MUSEUMS and restorations do not individually endorse products by name—a commercialism and a responsibility they prefer to avoid for reasons that are readily apparent. Ingredients may be changed without notice, and the right preparation can be used for the wrong job with disastrous results.

However, in querying curatorial staffs across the country, a majority reported using many of the same brands, which I am listing here as a convenience. (My own feeling is that while it is good to be told that a "mild" polish is best, you still need to know which specific item to take from the shelf.)

Product sources are given at the end of the chapter. Remember to read and follow manufacturers' directions carefully. Even the best product can sometimes be harmful when used incorrectly. If you have questions or doubts about using a preparation in a certain case, write to the manufacturer for guidance.

149

FOR WOOD

Paste waxes

>   Behlen's Blue Label Paste Wax
>
>   Butcher's Wax
>
>   Goddard's Cabinet Makers Wax
>
>   Hagerty's Vernax
>
>   Renaissance
>
>   Stair & Co.'s Stawax

Oils

>   Behlen's Acme Lemon Oil
>   Any pure lemon oil may be used, but with caution. Impurities in lemon oil can darken with age, but it is thought that modern reconstituted varieties avoid this problem.
>
>   Goddard's Teak Foam
>   Good for oil finishes on all woods, not just teak.

Other

>   Behlen's Scarid
>   Wax crayons in a range of eighty colors to fill in scratches. These are similar to children's crayons, but in wood colors and without abrasive impurities.
>
>   Goddard's Cabinet Makers Cloth
>   Soft cotton flannel impregnated with Goddard's Cabinet-maker's Wax—use for firearms, small items of leather or wood, or as a quick polish while you dust; excellent for wooden parts of upholstered furniture.

FOR METALS

Silver

Tarni-Shield by 3M Company
> The most frequently mentioned tarnish-retardant silver polish, it cleans and leaves a protective coating on silver. The company also recommends it as a mild cleaner for brass, solid gold, copper, and stainless steel, but it does not noticeably retard tarnish on these. It should *not* be used on gold plating, such as the inside of a silver cup or bowl, because it can be damaging to it.

Goddard's Silver Care Kit
> Combination polish and tarnish precentive.

Goddard's Long Shine Silver Polish
> Slightly longer-lasting protection against tarnish than with Goddard's Silver Care.

Goddard's Tarnish Preventive Spray
> A tarnish barrier that is not a lacquer, to be used if you decide upon the still longer-lasting tarnish protection of a spray.

Goddard's Long Shine Silver Cloth
> Cotton flannel cloth impregnated with polish and tarnish retardant, for quick touch-ups.

Goddard's Silver Brush
> A soft brush for cleaning crevices or ornamentation of silver and other metals.

Hagerty Silver Foam
> A mild polish, to be used with Mediterranean sponge also sold by Hagerty.

Hagerty Silversmiths' Wash
> Polish plus tarnish preventive to use with water wash.

Hagerty Silversmiths' Polish
Polish with tarnish preventive, no water necessary.

Hagerty Silversmiths' Gloves
Gloves treated with tarnish-preventive polish to use when dusting silver.

Hagerty Silver Spray
Not a lacquer, but a tarnish preventive to spray on as you dust silver.

International Silver Polish

Brass and Copper

Blue-Ribbon Brasso

Goddard's Shine Maker

Goddard's Shine Keeper
Liquid polish with added tarnish retardant for brass and copper.

Goddard's Glow Cloth
Impregnated cloth for quick polish of brass and copper. This is especially good for brass inlaid furniture, escutcheons, handles, or other hardware that must be polished against wood.

Hagerty Coppersmiths' Wash
Including a tarnish retardant for brass and copper.

Hagerty Copper & Brass Polish
Includes a tarnish preventive in a no-rinse formula, also sold with special sponge applicator.

Noxon
Although this polish is frequently listed by museums, there were a few reports that it was somewhat abrasive. You can dilute it with water, but my own feeling is that gentler polishes are better.

Pewter

Goddard's Pewter Care Kit

Hagerty Pewter Wash
Polishes for sliver, copper, and brass are also often used successfully for pewter.

Other Metals

Goddard's Glow
For brass, copper, stainless steel, pewter.

0000 steel wool
This finest grade is used occasionally—with great care—to polish rust off iron, steel, and tin. Most museums say they would never use it on pewter; some would use it to polish heavily blackened pewter—once—and if it were their own.

Tri-M-ite
An aluminum oxide paper used to take rust off iron, steel, and tin.

FOR TEXTILES

Orvus W. A. Paste
A safe detergent made by Proctor & Gamble. It is a viscous honeylike substance and is usually tested on a fabric in a solution of 10 percent Orvus to 90 percent water, then actual washing is done in a solution of 2 percent or 3 percent Orvus in water.

Igepal CA Extra
An alternate to the more frequently used Orvus.

Goddard's Carpet Cleaner

Goddard's Dry Clean
An aerosol spot remover.

Goddard's Wool Care
A warm-water wash that is nonshrinking; cold water sometimes doesn't remove soil well from old woolens.

Renuzit
Good all-purpose dry-cleaning solvent.

Other name-brand soaps and detergents for special purposes are listed in the chapter on Textiles.

FOR LEATHER

Fisher's British Museum Leather Dressing

Goddard's Saddlers Wax
Paste wax to nourish and polish leather.

Goddard's Saddlers Foam
Good cleaner for leather bindings, is said not to remove gold leaf.

Goddard's Shiner
Cleans and shines leather

Lexol
An emulsion for softening and flexing leather.

Talas Leather Protector
Approved British Museum formula with potassium lactate to protect leather from air pollution.

Talas Leather Dressing
Lanolin and neat's-foot oil according to a formula developed by the New York Public Library.

FOR MARBLE

Goddard's Marble Care Kit and Marble Polish

Calgon Detergent

FOR CHINA AND GLASS

Calgon Detergent

Ivory soap

SOURCES

Most of these products should be available in your local department, jewelry, or hardware stores. For those you are unable to locate, here are some mail-order sources:

Behlen's products
    Behlen Brothers
    10 Christopher Street
    New York, N. Y. 10014
    (Will only ship orders in some quantity since they are basically wholesale.)

Goddard's products
    J. Goddard & Sons Division
    S. C. Johnson & Son, Inc.
    1525 Howe St.
    Racine, Wisconsin 53403

Hagerty's products
    W. J. Hagerty & Sons, Ltd., Inc.
    South Bend
    Indiana 46624

Igepal CA Extra
    General Dyestuff Corp.
    435 Hudson Street
    New York, N. Y.

Stawax
    Stair & Co.
    59 East 57th Street
    New York, N. Y. 10022

Talas products + many more   Talas
104 Fifth Avenue
New York, N. Y.   10011
(This marvelous mail-order source ships in any amount. They carry Renaissance wax, their own leather dressings, Orvus W. A. Paste, acid-free mounting paper, rice and wheat pastes, antitarnish tissue papers, and a host of museum and library supplies. Write for their catalogue.)

ACKNOWLEDGMENTS

This book couldn't have been written at all without the kindness and help of curators, conservators, and their assistants from museums and restorations across the country. Their response in most cases was extraordinary, and I am grateful for their patience in answering my endless questions, and even more, for their generosity in sharing their hard-won expert knowledge.

I would also like to express my appreciation for the help of James C. Thornton of J. Goddard & Sons, Ltd., Gunner Thorp of Thorp Brothers, S. Dean Levy of Ginsburg & Levy, Inc., Robert Samuels, Jr., of French & Co., and Sir Humphrey Wakefield of Mallets at Bergdorf Goodman. My research was made easy by the exceptional staff of the Mamaroneck Free Library, and I am especially grateful to Lola Dudley and Miriam Baumann for their efforts in tracking down large numbers of elusive books. Both Helen Belknap, Librarian, and Jane Rittenhouse, Rare Books Librarian, gave valuable assistance when I worked in the Winterthur Museum Library. Thanks are due to Charles E. Overholser for his help in the early stages of research. And I am particularly indebted to Jane Wilson and Phoebe Larmore for encouraging me when it seemed I would never finish; to Jane Marion for doing much more than just typing the manuscript; and to William Whipple, for being a most understanding and excellent editor.

Above all, I want to thank the following institutions and individuals, without whose time and assistance this book would not have been possible:

Adena State Memorial Chillicothe, Ohio	Dard Hunter, Jr., Curator
The Bayou Bend Collection of The Museum of Fine Arts Houston, Texas	David B. Warren, Curator
Belle Meade Mansion Nashville, Tennessee	Mrs. B. E. Britt, Treasurer
The Bellingrath Home Theodore, Alabama	Margaret Taylor Moore, Executive Hostess
Birmingham Museum of Art Birmingham, Alabama	Richard F. Howard, Director
Bradford Brinton Memorial Big Horn, Wyoming	James T. Forrest, Director
The Brooklyn Museum Brooklyn, New York	Leon Rosenblatt, Conservator of Primitive Art Donald McHugh, Museum Technician Susanne P. Sack, Conservator of Paintings

Cohasset Historical Society— Historical Society Museum, Historic House, Maritime Museum Cohasset, Massachusetts	Mrs. Eleanor S. Marsh, Curator Emeritus and Advisory Director of the three museums
Colonial National Historical Park—Jamestown Museum, Yorktown Museum, Moore House Virginia	J. Paul Hudson, Head Curator
Colonial Williamsburg Foundation Williamsburg, Virginia	Staff
Cooper-Hewitt Museum of Decorative Arts & Design (a Smithsonian affiliate) New York, New York	Christian Rohlfing, Administrator
Delaware State Museum Dover, Delaware	Mrs. Roberta O. McClearnen, Curator
Essex Institute Salem, Massachusetts	Mrs. Huldah M. Payson, Curator of the Museum
The Frick Collection New York, New York	Edgar J. Munhall, Curator Theodore Dell
Wm. H. Harrison Mansion, "Grouseland" Vincennes, Indiana	Mrs. Lorethea Hamke, Curator
Hammond-Harwood House Annapolis, Maryland	Barbara C. Rouse, House Committee Chairman

Hampton National Historic Site Towson, Maryland	Mrs. D. L. McPherson, Jr., Resident Curator
Haverhill Historical Society Haverhill, Massachusetts	Samuel P. Horne, Treasurer
Hearst San Simeon State Historical Monument San Simeon, California	Ann Rotanzi, Supervisory Housekeeper and Custodian
Heritage Foundation Deerfield, Massachusetts	Mrs. Henry N. Flynt, Chairman of the Board of Trustees John S. Banta, Executive Director
Historic St. Augustine Preservation Board (and Pan American Museum) St. Augustine, Florida	Dr. Carleton I. Calkin, Curator
Historical Society of Old Newbury—Cushing House Newburyport, Massachusetts	Mrs. Ruth E. Walton, Curator
Independence National Historical Park Philadelphia, Pennsylvania	John C. Milley, Supervisory Curator
International Museum of Photography Rochester, New York	Robert Sobieszek, Assistant Curator, Research
Ipswich Historical Society—Whipple House Ipswich, Massachusetts	Mrs. Elizabeth H. Newton, Curator

Kenmore
  Fredericksburg, Virginia

Robert D. Burhans, Director

Litchfield Historical Society and
Museum
  Litchfield, Connecticut

William L. Warren, Director

Lyman Allyn Museum
  New London, Connecticut

Edgar deN. Mayhew, Director

Manchester Historic Association
  Manchester, New Hampshire

Mrs. Virginia G. Plisko, Director

Montclair Art Museum
  Montclair, New Jersey

Mrs. Elizabeth C. Miller,
  Preparator

Morristown National Historical
Park
  Morristown, New Jersey

T. C. Sowers, Museum Curator

The Mount Vernon Ladies'
Association
  Mount Vernon, Virginia

Miss Christine Meadows, Curator

Museum of American Folk Art
  New York, New York

Staff

Mystic Seaport Marine Historical
Association, Inc.
  Mystic, Connecticut

Revell Carr, Curator

Museum of Fine Arts
  Boston, Massachusetts

W. J. Young, Head of Research
  Laboratory

The Museum of the City of New York
New York, New York

Curatorial Staff
John Noble, Curator of the Toy Collection

National Park Service, Department of the Interior
Harpers Ferry, West Virginia

Miss Vera B. Craig, Staff Curator

National Trust for Historic Preservation
Washington, D. C.

Mrs. Leila J. Smith, Assistant to the Curator

Newport Historical Society
Newport, Rhode Island

Theodore E. Waterbury, Executive Director

North Carolina Museum of History
Raleigh, North Carolina

Dennis Walters, Jr., Conservator

New York State Historical Association
Cooperstown, New York

Per E. Guldbeck, Conservator
Caroline K. Keck, Sheldon Keck, Cooperstown Graduate Programs in Conservation of Historic and Artistic Works

---

Old Salem, Inc.
Winston-Salem, North Carolina

John Bivins, Jr., Curator of Crafts

Old Sturbridge Village
Sturbridge, Massachusetts

Henry J. Harlow, Chief Curator

Philadelphia Museum of Art Philadelphia, Pennsylvania	Theodor Siegl, Conservator Raymond Shepherd, Assistant Curator, Decorative Arts
Plymouth Antiquarian Society Plymouth, Massachusetts	Miss Rose T. Briggs, Curator
The Print Council of America Crown, New York	Theodore Gusten
Rock County Historical Society— Tallman Restorations Janesville, Wisconsin	Maureen McCarten, Collections Curator
Sandwich Glass Museum Sandwich, Massachusetts	Doris Kershaw, Director
The Shaker Museum Old Chatham, New York	Robert F. W. Meader, Director
Shelburne Museum, Inc. Shelburne, Vermont	Sterling D. Emerson, Director
Sleepy Hollow Restorations Irvington, New York	Joseph T. Butler, Curator Mrs. Gerard T. Monahan, Curatorial Department
Smithsonian Institution Washington, D. C.	Robert Organ, Chief of Conservation, Analytical Laboratory
The Society of the Founders of Norwich, Connecticut, Inc.— "The Leffingwell Inn" Norwich, Connecticut	Mrs. Jeanette Scheibner, Custodian Philip L. Johnson, President

Telfair Academy of Arts and
Sciences, Inc.
  Savannah, Georgia

Louis Cheney, Director

Textile Museum
  Washington, D. C.

Clarissa Palmai, Conservator
Colonel James W. Rice, Chemist
  Consultant

Tryon Palace
  New Bern, North Carolina

Miss Gertrude S. Carraway,
  Director

William Penn Memorial Museum
  Harrisburg, Pennsylvania

Eric de Jonge, Chief Curator

The William Trent House
  Trenton, New Jersey

Mrs. J. G. Gill, Hostess

Henry Francis du Pont Winterthur
Museum
  Winterthur, Delaware

Charles F. Hummel, Director
Jonathan Fairbanks, Conservator

BIBLIOGRAPHY

Grotz, George, *The Furniture Doctor.* Garden City, New York: Doubleday & Company, Inc., 1962.

Keck, Caroline K., *A Handbook on the Care of Paintings.* New York: Watson-Guptill Publications, 1965.

———— *How to Take Care of Your Pictures.* New York: Published jointly by the Museum of Modern Art and the Brooklyn Museum, 1954.

Luff, R. W. P., "The Problem of Furniture Restoration." *The Antique Collector,* June 1966.

Marsh, Moreton, *The Easy Expert in Collecting and Restoring American Antiques.* Philadelphia: J. B. Lippincott Co., 1959.

Morse, John D. (ed.), *Winterthur Conference Report 1969: Country Cabinet Work and Simple City Furniture.* Published for Henry Francis du Pont Winterthur Museum, Winterthur, Delaware. Charlottesville, Va.: University Press of Virginia.

Organ, R. M., *Design for Scientific Conservation of Antiquities.* Washington, D. C.: Smithsonian Institution Press, 1968.

Ormsbee, Thomas H., *Care and Repair of Antiques.* New York: Medill McBride Co., 1949.

Pienderleith, H. J., *The Conservation of Antiquities and Works of Art.* London: Oxford University Press, 1962.

Savage, George, *The Art and Antique Restorer's Handbook*. London: Rockliff Publishing Corp., 1954.

Some Notes on Atmospheric Humidity in Relation to Works of Art. London: Courtauld Institute of Art.

Zigrosser, Carl, and Gaehde, Christa M., *A Guide to the Collecting and Care of Original Prints*. Sponsored by The Print Council of America. New York: Crown, 1965.

INDEX

Accidents, possibility of, 9-10
Air-conditioning, 24, 53-54, 115
Alabaster, 117
Almond oil, 18, 26
Ambrotypes, 106-107
  cleaning of, 107
American Association of Watch Repairing, 118
American furniture, 13-14, 16
Antiques
  care of, 1-7
  family, 1, 3
  glorification of, 11
  knowledge of, 2-4
  living with, 8
  placement of, 22
  preventing damage to, 8-12
  protection of, 10-11
  use of, 12
Art Nouevau glass, 77
Ashtrays, 10

Bathing, in early days, 131-132
Bed hangings, 56, 65
Beeswax, 18

Beeton, Mrs., 134
Better Heating and Cooling Council, 23
Bindings
  leather, 114
  vellum, 114
Bloom, removal of, 24
Bobeches, 11
Bookworms, 114
Books, 113-115
  bindings of, 114-115
  care of, 114-115
  early, on household arts, 132-134
  mending of, 114-115
  pages of, 114
  shelving of, 114
Boston Museum of Fine Arts, 2, 20, 86
Brass, 46-50
  display of, 48
  do's and don'ts for, 50
  furniture, 48-49
  lacquering of, 48, 50
  list of polishes for, 152
  polishing of, 47

167

Breakage
  avoidance of, 10
  of china, 86
  glass, 79-80
  of mirrors and reverse painting,
    104
Brill, Robert, 76, 78-80
Brittania, 42-43
Bronze, 6, 46, 49-50
  do's and don't's for, 50
  gilt, 49
Bronze disease, 50
Brooklyn Museum, 84

Cabinetmakers, 14-15
Calkins, Carleton I., 32
Candle grease, removal of, 60
Candles, dripping, 11, 132
Caning, address for, 146
Carpet beetles, 71
Carpets, 69-73
  addresses of cleaners and re-
    pairers of, 138-139
  Aubusson, 70
  cleaning of, 71-72
  do's and don't's for, 73
  insects in, 71
  Oriental, 69-70, 72
  precautions in care of, 71
  spots and spills on, 71
  tears, rips, and worn spots in,
    70-71
  Turkey, 69, 129
Carr, Revell, 122
Ceramics, 82-88
  addresses for repair of, 146-147
Chandeliers
  addresses for cleaning of, 148
Cherry wood, 16
Chests, 10
China, 10, 82-88
  bone, 83

breakage of, 86
care of, 87
crazing on, 85, 88
decoration on, 85-86, 88
display of, 87-88
do's and don't's for, 88
glazed or unglazed, 84
list of cleaners for, 155
old, 88
  condition of, 84-85
  stains on, 85-86
  storage of, 87
  washing of, 84, 87-88
Cleaning materials, 149
  list of
    for china and glass, 155
    for leather, 154
    for marble, 154
  sources of, 155-156
Clocks, 117-119
  banjo, 117
  care of, 117-119
  grandfather, 117
  material used in, 117-118
  placement of, 119
  repair of, 118
    address for, 147
  winding of, 118
Cloth manufacture, 55-56
Collecting, arguments for, 8
Collectors, 1
Consumer Reports, 23
Cooper-Hewitt Museum, 56
Copper, 46-50
  display of, 48
  do's and don't's for, 50
  lacquering of, 48, 50
  list of polishes for, 152
  polishing of, 47
Corning Museum of Glass, 76-77,
    79, 81
Cosmetics, early, 131

Craig, Vera, 19
Crazing, 85
Cups, hanging of, 87
Currier & Ives lithographs, 91

Daguerreotypes, 90, 105-108
  cleaning of, 106
  frames and cases of, 107-108
  precautions for, 107-108
Damage, prevention of, 8-12
Dampness
  ivory and, 123
  old leather and, 115
  (*See also* Moisture)
Dealers, 3-4, 6
Decoys
  care of, 120-121
  repainting of, 121
  useful or decorative, 120
Defoe, Daniel, 134
Dehumidifying, 24, 53-54
Desks, 10
Detergents, 61-64, 66, 68, 153, 155
Documents, old, 117
Dolls, antique, care of, 112-113
Draperies, 56, 65-66
  addresses for cleaning of, 147-
    148
  care of, 66
Drawers, overstuffing of, 10
Dry cleaning, 56, 61-64, 139

Earnest, Adele, 121
Earthenware, 83
Elizabeth, Queen, 128, 131
Elizabethan period, 11, 69, 75

F. A. O. Schwartz, 111
Fabrics
  care of, 55-73
  do's and don't's for, 68-69
  fading of, 9, 65

mold on, 58
stains on, 58-59
  removal of, 59-64, 66
storage of, 57-58, 65-66, 69
tears or worn spots in, 58
upholstery, 14-15, 56
washing of, 61-64, 66-68
white, yellowing of, 69
Fading, 9, 65
  of rugs and carpets, 71
Fairbanks, Jonathan, 4, 6, 8, 19, 27
Figurines, 87
Fikioris, Mrs. Margaret, 65
Finger marks, prevention of, 11,
    53-54
Fireplaces, nearness to, 9, 46, 65
Floor coverings, 69-73
  do's and don't's for, 73
  early, 129
Flower receptacles, 10, 37, 42, 45,
    50, 80, 82, 88
Folk art, 90, 120
Forks, 128
Fracturs, 90
Framing of prints, 102
Franklin, Benjamin, 56
French furniture, 15-16, 49
Frick Collection, New York, 31
Fruitwoods, 16
Furniture, 1-3
  caning of, address for, 146
  cleaning of, 29-30
  debate on feeding of, 27-29
  marble tops on, 32-33
  painted, 16
  patina on, 5-6
    maintenance of, 13-30
  placement of, 22, 33, 132-133
  refinishing of, 3, 7, 15
  repair of, 14
    addresses for aid in, 144-146
    minor, 26-27

Furniture (*cont.*)
  restoration of, 14
  seventeenth-century, 129-130
  styles of, 13
  upholstery on, 14-15, 56, 129
Furniture brasses, 14
  addresses for makers of repro-
    ductions of, 146

Gaehde, Mrs. Christa, 99, 102-103
Giles, Mrs. Ashely, 111
Glass, 2, 75-82
  addresses for repair of, 147
  care of, 81-82
  display of, 80-81
  do's and don't's for, 82
  flint (lead), 76-77
  iridescent, 77
  list of cleaners for, 155
  popularity of, 75
  scratches, nicks, or breaks in, 79-
    80
  sedimentary deposits on, 78-80
  sick, 77-78
  storage of, 80
  transfer prints on, 90
Godey's Lady's Book, 91
Gold plate, 128
Gothic period, 13
Guldbeck, Per, 27
Guns, care of, 109-110

Harlow, Henry J., 93
Heat, excessive, avoidance of, 9, 46,
    65, 69, 85, 100, 114-115,
    119, 123
Heat pads, 10
Highboys, 10
Historic St. Augustine Preservation
    Board, 32
Horological Institute of America,
    118

House cleaning
  materials for, 131
  sixteenth-century, 129
Housekeeping, 135
  in early times, 125-135
    in America, 129
    in England, 127-128, 130, 134-
      135
    in France, 130
    in Italy, 126
  seventeenth-century, 129-130
  sixteenth-century, 129
Humidifiers, 23, 115
Humidity, 8-9
  for antique dolls, 113
  fabrics and, 58, 64, 69
  and ivory, 123
  oil paintings and, 91-92
  old books and, 114
  prints and, 100, 103
  relative, control of, 20-24, 33,
    120
  and silver storage, 40

Inlay, 17
International Museum of Photog-
    raphy, 106
Iron, 51-54
  cast, 51
  cleaning of, 51-52
  do's and don't's for, 54
  storage and maintenance of, 52-
    53
  wrought, 51, 53-54
Ivory, care of, 121-123

Jacobean period, 15
James I, 131
Japanning, 17

Karolik Collection, Boston, 2

Keck, Mrs. Sheldon, 91-92, 94, 96-97
Kennedy, John F., 121

Lacquer
on metal, 11, 39-40, 45, 48
on wood, 16-17
Leather
for book bindings, 114
care of, 115-116
decorations on, 116
list of cleaners for, 154
Lemon oil, 18, 24, 26, 150
Libraries, 4
Light, artificial, protection from, 99-100, 113
(*See also* Sunlight)
Lighting for oil paintings, 94, 98
Linseed oil, 16, 18, 27-30, 33, 53-54, 120
Louis XIV, 130
Lowboys, 10
Luxury, in early days, 130
Lymoff, 79

Mahogany, 16, 22
Mallet's of London, 9
Maple, 16
Maps, old, 117
Marble
list of cleaners for, 154
for tops on furniture, 32-33
Marquetry, 17
Meader, Robert, 86
Mechanical banks, care of, 110-111
Metal, 5
addresses for repair of, 148
care of, 1-3, 35-36
list of polishes for, 151-153
(*See also* kind of metal, as Silver)
Mildew, 113, 116

Mirrors, 90
backing of, 104
breaking of, 104
cleaning of, 104-105
Moisture
glass and, 81
oil paintings and, 92
repelling of, 10
and silver storage, 40-41
ways of maintaining in air, 21-22
Mold, 58, 69, 113, 116
Moth crystals, 57, 69
Moths, 57-58, 69, 71
Munhall, Edgar, 31
Museum of the City of New York, 111-113
Museum curators
addresses of services used by, 137-139
quoted, 2-3, 11-12, 14, 17-23, 27, 31, 40, 44, 53, 56, 59, 71, 76-80, 84, 86, 93, 106, 111, 122
Museum formula polish, 28
Mystic Seaport, 122

National Association of Watch and Clock Collectors, 118
National Institute of Dry Cleaners, 59
National Park Service, 19
New York State Historical Society, 27
Newport Historical Society, 19
Noble, John, 111-113
Norfolk, Duke of, 131

Oak, 15
Oberlin College, 137
Oil paintings, 7, 91-98
addresses for aid in cleaning of, 141-144

Oil paintings (*cont.*)
backing for, 92, 98
cleaning of, 93-96, 98
do's and don't's for, 97-98
expert treatment for, 91
lighting over, 94, 98
preservation of, 91-98
protection of, 93-95, 98
restoration of, 97-98
revarnishing of, 96
Oils
debate on use of, 27-29
for leather, 115-116
nondrying, 18, 120
and wax, 18-19
for wood, 150
(*See also* name of oil, as Linseed
oil)
Old Sturbridge Village, 93
Olive oil, 18, 24
Organ, Robert, 15, 20-21, 24, 27,
30
Orvus W. A. Paste, 64, 68, 153
Ownership, obligation of, 1

Pacific Cloth, 40
Paintings, 89-90
hanging of, 9-10, 92-93, 97-98
oil (*see* Oil paintings)
primitive, 89
reverse, 90, 104-105, 117-118
on wood, 92
Paper
addresses for aid in conservation
of, 140
book page, 114, 116
care of, 116-117
restoration of, 117
yellowing of, 117
Paraffin, 18
Parchment, 115

Pastels, 98-99
do's and don't's for, 103
Patina, 1, 12
on brass and copper, 47
on bronze, 49
cleaning and, 7
definition of, 5-6
protection of, 5
removal of, 6
on silver, 38, 40
of wood, maintenance of, 13-30
Pennsylvania Dutch art, 90
Pepys, Samuel, 130
Pewter, 42-46, 128
address for repair of, 148
do's and don't's for, 45-46
lacquering of, 45
list of polishes for, 153
polishing of, 43-46
sick, 43-44
Pewter polishes, 44-45
list of, 153
Philadelphia's Museum of Art, 40,
44, 53, 84
Pine, 16
Plate, 36
gold, 128
silver, 37, 128, 130-131
Plenderleith, H., 44
Polishes, 1-3, 17
French, 16
museum formula, 28
pewter, 44-45
silver, 38-39, 42
(*See also* Polishing materials)
Polishing
of brass and copper, 47
of pewter, 43-46
of silver, 38-39
of wood with linseed-oil finishes,
28-29

Polishing materials, 149
  early, 133
  list of, for metals, 151-153
    for wood, 150
  sources of, 155-156
Pompadour, Madame de, 130
Porcelain, 83-84, 86
  do's and don't's for, 88
  hard-paste, 83
  soft-paste, 83
Pottery, 83
Primitives, 89
Prints, 90-91, 98-103
  addresses for aid in conservation
    of, 140
  backing for, 100, 103
  care of, 102-103
  do's and don't's for, 103
  framing of, 102
  matting for, 100-101
  precautions for, 100-102
  rips in, 102-103
  spots on, 103
  unframed, 102
  warping and buckling of, 103

Queen Anne period, 15

Rawhide, 115
Refinishing of wood, 3, 7, 19-20, 33
Renaissance period, 13, 17
Renuzit, 19, 30, 64
Resilvering, 7
Reverse paintings, 90, 104-105
  breakage of, 104
  on clocks, 117-118
Rice, Colonel James W., 59, 72
Rohlfing, Christian, 56
Rosenblatt, Leon, 84
Rosewood, 16

Rugs, 69-73
  addresses of cleaners and repair-
    ers of, 138-139
  cleaning of, 71-72
  do's and don't's for, 73
  hooked braided, or rag, 70
  needlepoint, 70
  precautions in care of, 71
Rust, 51-52, 54

Salt, for stain removal, 59
Samplers, 90, 105
Scratches
  on glass, 79-80
  on wood, 25
Scrimshaw, 121-122
Servants, in early days, 132, 134
Shaker Museum, The, 86
Sheffield silver, 7, 37, 40-41
Shellac, 16-17
Shoe polish, for iron or tin, 53-54
Siegl, Theodore, 40, 44, 53, 84
Silhouettes, 90, 99
Silver, 5-7, 36-42
  addresses for repair of, 148
  American, 39
  care of, 36-38
  coin, 36
  and detergents, 38
  display of, 39-40, 42
  do's and don't's for, 42
  early, 128
  fire-scale on, 41
  identification marks on, 39
  lacquering of, 39-40
  patina on, 38, 40
  plated, 37, 128, 130-131
  polishing of, 38-39
  replating of, 41-42
  Sheffield, 7, 37, 40-41
  solid, 36-37

Silver (*cont.*)
  sterling, 36
  storage of, 40-42
  tarnishing of, 37-38
Silver polishes, 38-39
  list of, 151-152
  tarnish-preventive, 39, 42
Silverfish, 57, 69, 71
Smithsonian Institution, 15, 20, 24, 27, 30
Soaps, 60-64
  and water, 30
Sobieszek, Robert, 106
Soil removal chart, 61-63
South, the, care of furniture in, 24
Spode, 83
Spoons, 128
Spot removal, 62-63
  from prints, 103
  from rugs and carpets, 71
  from upholstery, 66
Stain removal, 59-64, 68-69
  all-purpose, 59-60
  chart of, 61-63
    definition of terms used in, 64
  from china, 85-86
  from leather, 116
Stains
  on china, 85-86
  on fabrics, 58-59
    blotting or ringing of, 60
  on leather, 116
Steel, 51
  cleaning of, 51-52
  do's and don't's for, 54
Stoddard's Solvent, 19, 30
Stoneware, 83
Stony Point Folk Art Gallery, 121
Sunlight, avoidance of, 9, 22-23, 65, 68, 71, 80-81, 103, 105, 107, 113, 117

Table linens
  in early days, 131-132
  storage of, 65-66
Tapestries, 65, 68
Tears
  in fabrics, 58
  in rugs and carpets, 70-71
Temperature, 8-9, 20, 22, 33
  for antique dolls, 113
  for fabrics, 65, 69
  and glass, 80
  ivory and, 123
  for oil paintings, 91-92
  for old books, 114
  pewter and, 46
  prints and, 100, 103
  for silver storage, 40-41
Textile Museum, Washington, D.C., 59, 72
Textiles, 55-69
  care of, precautions in, 65
    routine, 66-68
  do's and don't's for, 68-69
  hanging of, 65, 68
  identification of, 57
  list of cleaners for, 153-154
  mold on, 58
  stains of, 58-59
    removal of, 59-64, 66
  storage of, 57-58, 65-66, 69
  tears or worn spots in, 58
  washing of, 61-64, 66-68
Theorems, 90, 105
Tiles, 10
Tin, 51
  cleaning of, 51
  do's and don't's for, 54
  storage or maintenance of, 52-53
Tin pest, 43-44, 46, 53
Tintypes, 106-107
  cleaning of, 107
Toiles de Jouy, 56

Toys, antique, care of, 110-111
Transfer pictures, 90, 104-105
  breakage of, 104
Trivets, 10
Turpentine, 19

Upholstery, 14-15
  antique fabric, 56
    cleaning of, 66

Vacuuming
  of rugs and carpets, 71-72
  of textiles, 61, 66, 68
Valentines, 116
Varnish, 16-17
  bloom on, 24
Vellum, 114-115
Veneering, 17

Wakefield, Humphrey, 9
Wall cleaning, address for, 148
Walnut, 15
  burl, 15-16
Washing
  of china, 84, 87-88
  of ivory, 122-123
  of old dolls, 112-113
  of silver, 38-39
  of textiles, 61-64, 66-68
Water
  for china, 84
  to clean wood, 30
  soap and, 30, 84
Waterbury, Theodore, 19
Watercolors, 99
  do's and don't's for, 103
Waxes, 17-18, 53-54
  candelilla, 18
  carnauba, 18

cleaning, 25
microcrystalline, 17-18, 33
oil and, 18-19
paste, 26, 53, 120
  list of, 150
Waxing, of oiled pieces, 28-29
Wet-glass rings, 10, 25-26
  removal of, 26
Whatman, Susanna, 132
Williams, John, 132
Williamsburg, 9, 11, 65
Williamsburg's Housecleaning Manual, 47
Wilson, Kenneth, 77, 79-80
Winchester, Alice, 91
Windsor style, 16
Winterthur, 2, 4, 6, 8, 11, 19, 27, 65
Wood, 13-34
  cleaning of, 19, 29-30
  for clocks, 117
  colors of, 15, 22
  for decoys, 120
  do's and don't's for, 33-34
  finishes for, 16-19
  humidity, temperature and, 20-24
  kinds of, 2, 15-16
  paintings on, 92
  patina on, 6
    maintenance of, 13-34
  polishing materials for, 140
  routine care of, 31-32
  staining of, 15
Wood worm, 25
Worn spots
  in fabrics, 58
  in rugs and carpets, 70-71

Young, W. J., 20, 86